CIRIA REPORT 145                                   MARCH 1995

# CDM REGULATIONS - CASE STUDY GUIDANCE FOR DESIGNERS: AN INTERIM REPORT

CIRIA and CIC would welcome constructive comments arising from the experience of practitioners and ask that readers let David Churcher at CIRIA have their views as soon as possible. CIRIA and CIC hope that it will be possible to issue an updated revision when sufficient experience in the application of the Regulations has accumulated.

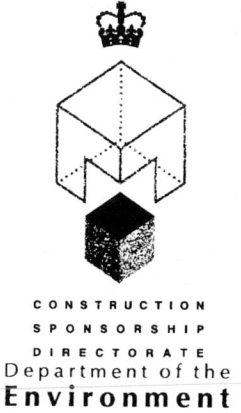

CONSTRUCTION
SPONSORSHIP
DIRECTORATE
Department of the
Environment

Construction Industry Council

CIRIA

CONSTRUCTION INDUSTRY RESEARCH AND INFORMATION ASSOCIATION
6 Storey's Gate, Westminster, London SW1P 3AU
Tel 0171-222 8891                              Fax 0171-222 1708

# Summary

The Construction (Design & Management) Regulations 1994 (the CDM Regulations) will impose statutory duties on clients, designers and contractors and introduce the roles of planning supervisor and principal contractor. The Regulations provide the framework for managing the issues of health and safety during the construction, repair, maintenance and demolition of civil engineering, building and engineering construction works.

One of the features of the Regulations and the associated Approved Code of Practice (ACOP) is the fresh emphasis they lay on the importance of considering health and safety aspects of construction during the various phases of designing a project.

This publication provides guidance on the application of CDM Regulation 13 'Requirements on designer'. It is, therefore, addressed to designers and design organisations, in particular their handling of health and safety issues as a design consideration and their inputs to the pre-tender stage health and safety plan and file. Eight examples illustrate this role for a range of architectural, building and civil engineering projects with a wide variety of health and safety hazards. The examples have been prepared by designers with professional experience as architect, building surveyor, building services engineer, civil engineer and structural engineer.

This publication does not offer complete guidance on all aspects of the Regulations and designers are urged to study the full texts of the Regulations and ACOP and refer also to guidance available from the Health and Safety Executive such as *Designing for health and safety in construction* and *A guide to the managing of health and safety in construction*.

**CDM Regulations - case study guidance for designers: an interim report**
*Construction Industry Research and Information Association*
CIRIA Report 145, 1995

**Keywords**
Construction (Design & Management) Regulations, health and safety plan, health and safety file, design, designers

**Reader Interest**
Construction industry designers, architects, civil engineers, structural engineers, services engineers, surveyors, consultants, local authorities

| CLASSIFICATION | |
| --- | --- |
| AVAILABILITY | Unrestricted |
| CONTENT | Guidance |
| STATUS | Committee guided |
| USER | Construction sector designers |

© CIRIA 1995                                    ISBN 0 86017 421 2

Published by CIRIA, 6 Storey's Gate, Westminster, London SW1P 3AU. All rights reserved. No part of this publication may be reproduced or transmitted in any form or by any means, including photocopying and recording, without the written permission of the copyright holder, application for which should be addressed to the publisher. Such written permission must also be obtained before any part of this publication is stored in a retrieval system of any nature.

# Foreword

With the coming into force of the Construction (Design and Management) Regulations (CDM) designers have new health and safety duties and opportunities. They will now be able to play their part in tackling the unacceptably high rates of death, injury and ill-health associated with work in the construction industry.

I welcome this report. It will help designers to understand what practical steps they can take to comply with CDM. The report makes clear that innovative designers need not fear the Regulations, but they do need to apply their skills to the consideration of health and safety problems to a greater extent than has been general practice up to now.

This report provides much useful information. Designers will be well equipped to tackle CDM if they read this report together with the Regulations and the other guidance which is available. This guidance includes the Approved Code of Practice and the two Construction Industry Advisory Committee (CONIAC) guidance documents, *Designing for health and safety in construction* and *A guide to managing health and safety in construction*.

Some of the assumptions the authors have had to make in these early case studies may require review as the knowledge of CDM grows. CIRIA and HSE are committed to developing and expanding the body of information available to assist designers with their CDM duties. I am keen to foster links with the professions and a second joint project involving designers and, in addition, contractors in identifying the hazards associated with different work sections will soon get under way. This will provide a valuable aide memoire for designers to highlight the issues they should consider.

I believe that studies such as these will provide a stimulus for the industry to come together to tackle its poor health and safety record. Without effort by all those involved in the construction process the problems of death, injury and ill-health in the industry will never be resolved.

This report illustrates how designers' considerations of health and safety issues fit into the design process and I commend it to you.


**STUART NATTRASS**
**HM Chief Inspector of Construction**
**Health and Safety Executive**

# Preface

The Construction (Design & Management) Regulations 1994 (the CDM Regulations) have been prepared by the Health and Safety Executive (HSE) to transpose the European Community's *Temporary and Mobile Construction Sites Directive* (92/57/EEC). They will impose statutory duties on clients, designers and contractors and introduce the roles of planning supervisor and principal contractor.

A consultative document incorporating the draft Regulations and the Approved Code of Practice (ACOP) was distributed by the HSE in October 1992. Extensive comment was received from the construction industry and the Construction Industry Council (CIC) appointed a Task Force under the chairmanship of Professor Donald Bishop to represent the interests of construction professionals and to liaise with the HSE.

This CIRIA publication was prepared as the Regulations and ACOP were being finalised for Ministerial approval on the basis of the drafts dated 7 February 1994. The report was also checked against the Regulations laid before Parliament on 10 January 1995. Account was taken of *Designing for health and safety in construction*, a document prepared under the guidance of HSC's Construction Industry Advisory Committee (CONIAC), (draft dated 31 May 1994).

The design professions have expressed wide ranging concerns about the Regulations, particularly with respect to the new duties and responsibilities they impose. Some design practices have been working towards incorporating CDM in their existing systems and procedures for some time, although the large majority, especially smaller practices with fewer resources, have not been able to do this. It was therefore in the interests of all professional designers for CIRIA and CIC to co-operate to produce the guidance contained in this publication.

The full meaning and significance of the Regulations, interpreted by the ACOP, will only emerge as they are applied in practice and (perhaps) tested in the courts. Organisations in the construction sectors will wish to ensure that they comply with the Regulations and it is expected that this publication will provide helpful information for designers on how the requirements of the CDM Regulations may be satisfied, with other guidance coming from the HSE and private sector organisations. As will be clear to the reader, this publication does not (indeed could not) offer complete guidance on all aspects of the Regulations and designers are urged to study the full texts of the Regulations and the ACOP for themselves, as well as other guidance documents.

**Collaboration**

The project leading to the publication of this report was undertaken by CIRIA in collaboration with the Construction Industry Council (CIC).

**Authors**

The drafting of the eight examples (Sections 4-11) was carried out by the individuals listed below. These inputs were provided as contributions-in-kind to the project to an extremely tight timetable and CIRIA is very grateful to the authors and their employers for all their efforts - the publication could not have appeared without them.

| Author | Organisation | Section drafted |
|---|---|---|
| Mr J Crooks | D Y Davies Associates | 4 |
| Mr G Briffa | Briffa Phillips | 5 |
| Mr K Dew | John Pelling & Partners | 6 |
| Mr D Watson | WSP Consulting Engineers | 7 |
| Mr M Stokes | L G Mouchel & Partners Ltd | 8 |

| Mr A Delves | Ove Arup Partnership | 9 |
| Mr P Gray | Scott Wilson Kirkpatrick & Partners | 10 |
| Mr I Neil | ACER Group Ltd | 11 |

The professional background of each author is listed in Section 3.

**Project Steering Group**

The work was guided by a Steering Group which advised on the content of the report, reviewed the drafts of the report during the research period and approved the text of this publication. CIRIA wishes to express its appreciation for the work done by members of the Project Steering Group in committee and in commenting on drafts.

| Professor D Bishop (Chairman) | CIC Health and Safety Task Force |
| Mr J Burkett | Chartered Architect |
| Mr S Bell | RIBA, CONIAC |
| Mr D Brown | Steel Construction Institute |
| Mr W A Heron | AMEC Civil Engineering Ltd |
| Mr D Hunter/Mr J Williams | Rust Consulting Ltd |
| Mr D Lamont/Mr N Thorpe | Health and Safety Executive |
| Dr M Lockwood | Construction Industry Council |
| Mr B Mansell | ICE Safety Panel, CONIAC |
| Mr R Oughton | FC Foreman & Partners |
| Mr J Read | WS Atkins Consultants Ltd |
| Mr M Stokes | Institution of Structural Engineers (L G Mouchel & Partners Ltd) |
| Mr M Tucker | formerly Laing Construction |
| Mr J Veal | Royal Institute of British Architects |
| Mr G Ventris/Mr E Cobb | Health and Safety Executive |
| Mr P Williams | The British Constructional Steelwork Association |
| Mr P Winstone | Watts and Partners |
| | |
| Mr D W Churcher | CIRIA |
| Dr D E Wright | Consultant CIRIA |

**Finance**

The project was supported financially by the DoE Construction Sponsorship Directorate, the Health and Safety Executive and CIRIA's Core Programme. As noted above, contributions-in-kind given by the organisations and individuals involved in drafting the examples were a key factor in enabling CIRIA to start the project quickly.

# Status of report

This report has been prepared to give preliminary guidance to designers of civil engineering and building works on how to meet their responsibilities under the recently introduced CDM Regulations.

In each example, key health and safety issues, hazards and risks have been identified and discussed and some of the designer's contributions to the pre-tender stage health and safety plan and file are described. The guidance given does not purport to define legal liabilities, nor does it pretend to be exhaustive. It is offered to the professions associated with construction to illustrate the way in which informed designer opinion now believes that the Regulations and Approved Code of Practice will be applied.

Readers are advised that, while the advice conveyed in this publication is believed to conform with the CDM Regulations and Approved Code of Practice, in advance of the testing of these documents in the courts, no reliance can be placed upon the advice as being applicable to any particular circumstance.

# Revision of interim report

It is expected that this publication, as well as providing basic guidance to designers, will promote further discussion and debate regarding the interpretation and application of the CDM Regulations. It has therefore been issued as an interim report.

Considering that:

- the CDM Regulations are new and there is some uncertainty about the precise meaning and legal implications of the Regulations and Code

- the responsibilities on designers as now expressed in the Regulations and ACOP are new

- the worked examples are innovative, and

- only experience will establish the level of detail needed to ensure that the pre-tender stage health and safety plan and health and safety file are sufficient and relevant

the use of the guidance contained in this interim report by construction professionals is certain to identify many matters which will require revision/correction/expansion.

# Contents

# List of Figures

# List of Tables

# 1    Introduction

## 1.1    THE PURPOSE, SCOPE AND LIMITATIONS OF THIS REPORT

This report has been produced to assist designers to understand the need for information to be provided to go into the health and safety plan and file as a consequence of the Construction (Design & Management) Regulations 1994[1] and to illustrate the type of information that will be required.

It presents eight case studies of different projects, of different sizes, work types and each written by a single designer as examples of how the Regulations impact on the design and information production process. These case studies have been produced by CIRIA, in collaboration with the Construction Industry Council, and representatives from professional institutions, design practices and health and safety consultants, to complement the existing guidance available from HSE. The case studies are aimed at practising designers and have been written to cover only the period of a project prior to the appointment of a contractor. Each case study shows how the project design process can incorporate the rationale for rigorous health and safety consideration that is required by the CDM Regulations.

The CDM Regulations are new, although some of the duties they impose on designers were implicit in Section 3 of the Health and Safety at Work etc. Act 1974. The requirements are set out in the Regulations, while guidance on their application is set out in the Approved Code of Practice (ACOP).

The examples contained in this report are not prescriptive, but indicative. Some examples are based on real projects, others are fictitious. They are breaking new ground and to that extent the whole study is innovative. Perhaps most important of all, the examples represent what responsible designers and CIRIA's widely representative project steering group believe the Regulations and ACOP actually mean in practice and how they can be applied in a range of construction situations.

It is also important for readers to appreciate that the guidance given in the examples cannot be complete. Some particular features of the health and safety hazards of each case have been selected as key issues and discussed in more detail. Other aspects have been outlined, while yet others would have been identified and discussed in detail had the examples been done as an actual project.

These reservations accepted, HSE, CIRIA and CIC are aware that the guidance contained in this report could help to define what the Regulations and Code mean in a de facto sense and trust that the case studies will be helpful to all designers when they set out to respond to the Regulations.

## 1.2    DOCUMENTS AND GUIDANCE AVAILABLE FROM HSE

This report MUST be read in association with the following documents available from the Health and Safety Executive:

1.    The Approved Code of Practice which incorporates the Regulations themselves
2.    Designing for Health and Safety in Construction (CONIAC guidance document for designers available from HSE)

---

[1] Statutory Instrument 1994/3140

3. A Guide to Managing Health and Safety in Construction (CONIAC guidance)
4. The Management of Health and Safety at Work Regulations 1992, which are also covered by the ACOP.

The Regulations are the statutory instrument transposing the original EC Directive, *The implementation of minimum health and safety requirements at temporary or mobile construction sites (92/57/EEC)* into UK legislation.

The ACOP, whilst not a statutory instrument, is much more than an advisory document, insofar as it gives the official interpretation of the Regulations. The following is taken from the ACOP:

> "This code has been approved by the Health and Safety Commission and gives advice on how to comply with the law. This code has a special legal status. If you are prosecuted for breach of health and safety law, and it is proved that you have not followed the relevant provisions of the code, a court would find you at fault, unless you can show that you have complied with the law in some other way."

*Designing for Health and Safety in Construction*, drafted by the Health and Safety Executive, approved by the Construction Industry Advisory Committee (CONIAC) and published by the Health and Safety Commission, provides the official guidance regarding the duties and responsibilities of designers.

## 1.3 WHAT ARE THE CDM REGULATIONS?

The Construction (Design and Management) Regulations will impose statutory duties on clients, designers and contractors and introduce the roles of planning supervisor and principal contractor. They have a very positive purpose - to reduce the toll of accidents and damage to the health of all "at work" in the industry.

The principal objectives of the Regulations include the following:

• to promote proper consideration and the better management and co-ordination of health and safety issues throughout every phase of construction, including concept, outline and detailed design, maintenance, repair, cleaning and demolition

• to require designers to include adequate regard to the health and safety of persons at work carrying out "construction work or cleaning" (as defined by the Regulations) or of any other person who might be affected by the work among other design considerations

• to create two documents: the first is the health and safety plan which is prepared in two stages, (prior to and following the appointment of a contractor), and is used to convey health and safety information to the contractor during the tender and construction phases of the project; the second is the health and safety file - this holds information about health and safety matters which will assist those carrying out construction, maintenance, repair or demolition work on a structure at any time after the completion of the project.

For a complete description of the Regulations and their interpretation, readers should refer to the published ACOP and Regulations. In particular, attention is drawn to the definitions in regulation 2 (1) of, inter alia, construction work, design, designer, project and structure.

# 2 Effects of the CDM Regulations on the role of a designer

While not reducing the responsibilities of contractors for health and safety during construction, the Regulations extend traditional responsibilities to include designers in the belief that many decisions made in the planning phase of a construction project can have a direct influence on safety on site. The following parts of this section show how the requirements of the Regulations and the guidance given in the ACOP have been illustrated in the case studies. Sections 2.7 and 2.8 describe the health and safety plan and file respectively and Section 2.9 summarises the duties of planning supervisors with respect to designers.

## 2.1 CDM AND THE STAGES OF A NORMAL PROJECT - DESIGNER'S FUNCTIONS

The case studies in this document consider the different design stages of a project and the functions of designers in relation to CDM during these stages.

### 2.1.1 Feasibility

Regulation 13, which places duties on designers, applies to any design the designer prepares and which he is aware will be used for the purposes of construction work. It was the view of the Project Steering Group that this included feasibility studies and that it would be right and prudent to take health and safety considerations into account when making the strategic decisions that often characterise these studies.

### 2.1.2 Design prior to the appointment of a contractor

This part of a project is typically divided into several design stages (concept, outline, scheme, detailed), depending on the project and the nature of the work:

1. Concept/outline design

Designers may make significant contributions to health and safety at these early stages. When options are open, potential hazards which are identified can often be designed out with little or no disruption or cost.

> Example: Section 9 (Bridge project) - the concept stage identified that working over the railway and river will be hazardous if in-situ construction is used. The detailed design used prefabricated deck units, as a consequence.

Information regarding the site features known to the designer and the strategic design decisions made during the concept design stage are relevant inputs to the health and safety plan and the health and safety file, as appropriate.

2. Scheme/detailed design

Designers carry forward the strategic decisions made previously and have to consider both the potential hazards which have not been eliminated during the concept or outline design stages and the hazards which have arisen from a more detailed development of the design.

The principles of prevention and protection (see Section 2.6) are used to eliminate, reduce or control the risks to site workers.

> Example: Section 5 (New build architectural project) - the scheme design stage identifies that silicate dust will be a hazard through chasing brickwork for service conduits. It is therefore decided to use dry lining to eliminate this hazard. In addition, beam and pot floors are specified rather than precast slabs to take advantage of smaller and more manageable components. A further advantage of this decision is it avoids the need for a large crane to be used on the congested site.

The actual division between design stages will, of course, depend on the nature of the project. The principle that is being demonstrated is that as the design progresses from concept to detail, the integral consideration of health and safety issues also changes from general to specific. As the design progresses and becomes more and more fixed, health and safety considerations necessarily have to focus more and more closely on actual site operations and situations.

Information regarding the decisions made by the designers will be stored in the health and safety plan and/or the health and safety file, as appropriate. The planning supervisor has the duty to ensure that the health and safety plan is prepared but the Regulations do not specify who is to actually compile the plan. The planning supervisor also has the duty to ensure the file is prepared and then has the duty to review, amend or add to the file throughout the project. In either case, a lot of the information for these documents will originate from designers.

Both the health and safety plan and the health and safety file are live documents, that is they are updated and amended during the design process and also during the construction stage as more detailed or different information becomes available.

> Example: This is shown in Section 7 (Refurbishment of building services) - at the concept design stage, information is provided that identifies the removal and disposal of existing services and plant as a hazard. At the outline stage, this information has been modified to take account of the results of an asbestos survey, removal of pipework, ductwork, light fittings and the clearing of galvanised steel cisterns.

At all stages, the purpose of the health and safety plan and file are to identify hazards that are significant or unusual in the circumstances of the project. When deciding what information to provide for subsequent inclusion in the plan and/or the file, the designer has to assume that the contractor will be competent to deal with commonplace hazards and judge accordingly.

> Example: Section 6 (Overcladding tower block) - in the assessment of options for improving the windows, the designer considers that neither option offers significant health and safety advantages. The chosen option to renew with double glazed units is in itself assessed as being routinely carried out by competent contractors and the references put in the plan and file relate to the particular circumstances of this project - difficult access, interface with occupants, etc. and the need for a contractor to provide a method statement of how he intends to ensure this is achieved safely.

### 2.1.3  Procurement stage

Under standard contractual arrangements, with contractors selected by the normal competitive tender process, there is very little for the designer to do specifically related to CDM duties, unless he is involved either in the pre-selection or appointment of contractors.

In this case, there is a duty to be satisfied that any contractor appointed is competent to do the work. Judging this will include referring to the health and safety plan which forms part of the tender documentation and the tenderers' responses to it in their submissions.

However, regulation 13(1) requires designers to take reasonable steps to ensure that the client is aware of his own duties under the CDM Regulations.

### 2.1.4 Construction stage

The contractor remains entirely responsible for health and safety on site and on a traditional contract the designer has little to do as far as the CDM Regulations are concerned. However, the live nature of the health and safety plan and the health and safety file means that the planning supervisor or whoever has the responsibility for maintaining these documents will request further information in the event of design variations. This aspect is not demonstrated in the case studies as they have been written to cover only the pre-construction stage.

## 2.2 EFFECT OF DUTIES IN CDM ON MANAGEMENT OF THE DESIGN PROCESS

It is important to emphasise that the imposition of the CDM Regulations need not cause any designers to do much more than good design and good design management already imply. Risk assessment is a new area for some types of work. This has given rise to some concern, which will take time to resolve as experience accumulates.

The use of design reviews and the existence of design notes for internal record-keeping purposes will mean that most of the management systems for coping with CDM duties are already in place. The Regulations introduce some new aspects to this work, to co-operate with the planning supervisor with regard to health and safety issues which will mean providing suitable information to him and also to whoever is charged with preparing and maintaining the plan and preparing the file. This will have the effect of formalising the process of record keeping to produce an audit trail for decision making which can be referred to in the event of any query.

## 2.3 CO-OPERATION WITH OTHER DUTY HOLDERS

As is noted above, the CDM Regulations impose a duty on designers to co-operate with the planning supervisor. Also in regulation 13 (2) (c) is a duty to co-operate with other designers on the same project, where there is an overlap or interface in health and safety issues.

Example: Section 4 (Refurbishment project) - a list of hazards is identified and developed through the different design stages. At the appropriate time, an assessment is made as to whether these are best addressed by the architect, who is the designer in question for this case study, or by another design team member. Those which are best handled by another designer are handed over, and noted as such in the architect's records. The planning supervisor is also kept informed and these hazards are not featured in the architect's own risk assessments.

## 2.4 NON-CONVENTIONAL PROJECTS

In non-conventional projects, the development of the health and safety plan and file will follow the design process. Where the project work is being let as a number of work packages, each with their specialist tender information, the health and safety plan will also be prepared in packages. There will, however, be some parts of the plan which are general and will apply to all work packages, e.g. those dealing with the site as a whole. The specific parts of each plan will identify the remaining hazards in the design which are pertinent to that particular item of work.

Example: Section 4 (Refurbishment project) - the example health and safety plan prepared to illustrate the inputs made by the architect, in this case, has been developed for two different work packages, demolition and brickwork. At appropriate parts of the plan, alternative sections are shown for each of these, which would be included at that point for each respective document.

## 2.5 EXEMPTED PROJECTS

The CDM Regulations do not apply in the same way to all construction projects. According to work type, project duration or human resource requirements, the separate duty holders have different duties. This is explained fully in the CONIAC guidance *Designing for health and safety in construction* and reference should also be made to *A guide to managing health and safety in construction*.

## 2.6 THE PRINCIPLES OF PREVENTION AND PROTECTION

The Principles of Prevention and Protection set out in the CDM and Management of Health and Safety at Work Regulations ACOPs provide an ordered methodology for the consideration of the reduction of health and safety risks to those working on site. Not all of them are relevant to what a designer can do. The design requirements of CDM, in regulation 13, which are derived from the principles refer to the need to:

* avoid foreseeable risks (i.e. eliminate the hazard, if possible, by changing the design)

* combat risks at source (i.e. reduce the risks from the hazards that remain)

* give priority to measures which will protect all persons affected by the works rather than the individual at work (e.g. prefer walkways with handrails to safety harnesses).

The designer has to give adequate regard to these needs among the design considerations. An integral part of a designer's function when evaluating the balance between the other considerations and the health and safety of construction workers is to carry out risk assessment. As the design develops, the designer should examine methods by which the structure might be built and analyse the hazards and risks associated with these. The appropriate level of risk assessment will vary from project to project. Where there are major hazards a detailed analysis may be needed. But often a simply qualitative judgement based on the seriousness of an incident that would otherwise result will be sufficient. This is largely a new area for designers and the issues are reviewed in Section 12.

The designer is not expected to take responsibility for all risks that will eventually arise on site. Designers are required to avoid etc. such risks only to the extent it is reasonable to expect them to address the risks at the time the design is prepared and to the extent it is otherwise reasonably practicable to do so. The ACOP makes it clear that health and safety is not expected to prevail at the cost of all else. But it must be appreciated that these requirements are driven by the understanding that risk avoided and reduced in design is more reliably dealt with than it ever could be by management on site.

Example: If the need for access at height can be eliminated in design, or if access could safely be provided within the structure being designed, the matter would not require all the effort necessary to produce the same level of safety with scaffolding: expense, safe erection by trained and supervised staff, regular examination etc.

The availability of such standard techniques to the contractor reduces the weight given by the designer to the case for avoidance or reduction of risks in the balance of design considerations.

It must be remembered that contractors, as employers of site workers, are required to observe a considerable body of law directed to the management and control of the risks they are faced with. Designers are able to take this into account when providing information for the plan and file. With this in mind, it will not be necessary to provide volumes of standard information which would have the effect of obscuring that relating to salient, non standard or possibly unexpected health and safety hazards and risks. However, any assumptions made by a designer regarding the competence of a contractor or the use of a standard method should be stated to reduce any room for disagreement.

## 2.7 THE HEALTH AND SAFETY PLAN

The preparation of the health and safety plan and the health and safety file (see Section 2.8) are activities which are not specifically part of a designer's duties. However, since one of the purposes of these documents is to pass design information to other parties, all designers must have a degree of involvement in them.

Given the above, it is important that designers are made aware of the type of information that will be required, since they may have to produce it or will certainly be involved in its production.

Each of the case studies concludes with a health and safety plan prepared according to regulation 15 (1)-(3). There is no convenient shorthand to describe this document defined in the Regulations, and this report has adopted the terminology "pre-tender stage health and safety plan". This is the document that is available at the end of the traditional design process to be included in tender information for potential contractors. Each case study also lists the contents of the health and safety file. The structures of the plan and file are based upon the ACOP Appendices 4 and 5 respectively.

### 2.7.1 The pre-tender stage health and safety plan

The health and safety plan should be sufficiently developed to form part of the tender documentation. It will then:

- make plain the health and safety issues specific to the project

- note where and when the principal risks are likely to occur and alert tenderers to hazards that may be unexpected in the circumstances of the project, thus enabling all to take these into account when tendering and to plan safe systems of work

- provide clients with a parameter against which to judge that they are selecting competent and properly resourced contractors by assessment of their responses to the plan, and thus

- eliminate contractors who have failed to demonstrate that they will plan and provide resources for work to be done safely.

The areas in which the health and safety plan gives information are described in Appendix 4 to the ACOP.

Much of the information to be included may already be provided elsewhere in the tender documentation. The ACOP makes it clear that the health and safety plan must be aligned to the scale and complexity of the project in hand. There is no policy intention that health and safety plans should duplicate information from elsewhere in the tender documents when references can be given. As noted in Section 2.9, although the planning supervisor has a duty to ensure the health and safety plan is prepared, instruction for its actual preparation has to be given by the client.

### 2.7.2 The development of the health and safety plan during the construction stage

Responsibility for the health and safety plan is transferred from the planning supervisor to the principal contractor as soon as possible after his appointment. The contractor has to update, implement and, as necessary, modify such plans. In most circumstances health and safety plans will evolve continuously as construction progresses and as sub-contractors' health and safety risk assessments are absorbed. The plan will also take account of any design changes.

The health and safety plan ceases to have any function when the construction stage of the project is complete.

## 2.8 THE HEALTH AND SAFETY FILE

The Foreword to the ACOP states "the health and safety file amounts to a normal maintenance manual enlarged to alert those who will be responsible for a structure after handover to risks that must be managed when the structure and associated plant is maintained, repaired, renovated or demolished. It is a record of information to inform future decisions on the management of health and safety." Although the Regulations and ACOP do not specify a format for the files, an indicative contents list is given in Appendix 5 to the ACOP.

One purpose of the file is to enable future planning supervisors to take account of potential health and safety problems inherent in the structure and to ensure reference to them in future health and safety plans. As such the health and safety file will then inform designers and contractors working on the structure at a later date.

It is difficult to be precise about what should be placed on the file in addition to normal as-built record drawings and maintenance manuals. There is obviously a risk of it becoming a "dustbin" and containing so much material that it becomes virtually unusable.

All the information put onto the file must be relevant to future work on the structure. Thus it should include information on construction methods and materials used, fire precautions, the location of services, the operation, repair and maintenance of plant and maintenance schedules for the constructed facilities. Special attention should be paid to matters like load paths, structures that are unstable at intermediate stages of dismantling, potentially toxic materials and so on.

It is the planning supervisor's responsibility to ensure that the file is prepared (as for the plan) and where there are two or more designers, that their inputs are co-ordinated. Contractors also have a duty to provide relevant information to the planning supervisor. The planning supervisor retains responsibility for the file throughout the project and is responsible for delivering it to the client on completion.

It can be seen that proper completion of the file will discharge some or all of the duties of a planning supervisor with respect to health and safety plans in future projects concerning the maintenance, refurbishment or demolition of the works.

## 2.9 THE PLANNING SUPERVISOR

Although this report does not attempt to provide guidance on the role of the planning supervisor, it is important that designers understand the functions and duties of the planning supervisor and the following is included for completeness:

The duties of planning supervisors as they relate to designers are set out in regulations 14 and 15 (1)-(3) and explained in more detail in the ACOP paragraphs 69-81 & 86 & 87. In summary, they are responsible for ensuring:

- that a health and safety plan is prepared before arrangements for carrying out or managing the construction work are completed

- that, as far as is reasonably practicable, the design includes adequate regard for designer's duties under regulation 13 (2) (a) and adequate information

- co-operation by designers, as far as is reasonably practicable

- they are in a position to give advice

- that a health and safety file is prepared, which they then keep up to date during the project and ensure is passed to clients on completion of the project.

# 3 Nature of the report

## 3.1 CASE STUDY EXAMPLES

This study is based around eight examples described in Sections 4 to 11, each indicating the scope of the designer's responsibility under the new CDM Regulations. They incorporate a range of architectural, building and civil engineering projects. The number of examples included was the result of a balance between covering a representative range of work types and producing a reasonably concise report. Each example was written from the point of view of a specific member of the design team.

The topics and design team professions were:

| Section | Topic | Approximate value £M | Design viewpoint for case study |
|---------|-------|----------------------|---------------------------------|
| 4. | Refurbishment project | £3.0M | Architect |
| 5. | New build project | £0.2M | Architect |
| 6. | Tower block overcladding during occupation | £0.75M | Building Surveyor |
| 7. | Refurbishment of building services | £1.7M | Building Services Engineer |
| 8. | Structure for superstore | £8.5M | Structural Engineer |
| 9. | Bridge project | £0.25M | Civil Engineer |
| 10. | Retaining wall project | £1.5M | Civil Engineer |
| 11. | Tunnel project | £100M | Civil Engineer |

The names of authors and their firms are given in the Preface.

All praise must be given to the authors who freely agreed to make an interpretation of the draft Regulations and the ACOP by setting out the assessments and contributions they might have made to the health and safety plan and file in practice. Whilst designers may occasionally explain the objects pursued and compromises made when reaching general design solutions, few do so in the detail necessary for others to understand their assessment of strategic issues. This the authors have done. Consequently the length of the case studies is much greater than that needed merely to state, assess and keep track of the health and safety issues.

## 3.2 APPROACH ADOPTED IN THE EXAMPLES FOR THE PREPARATION OF A PRE-TENDER STAGE HEALTH AND SAFETY PLAN

The examples illustrate the consideration given by this group of designers to selected health and safety issues during the design process. That consideration extends to all persons employed in or affected by the construction, maintenance, repair and eventual demolition of the works. It is assumed in the examples that designers are sufficiently aware of other statutory legislation applicable to construction activities or are able to obtain advice from "competent sources".

The CDM Regulations mechanism of passing a health and safety plan from design to construction has been reflected in the design process and also adopted between each design stage. In each example health and safety issues and associated hazards are reassessed if applicable at each design stage. For each one the text is divided into two: the first part contains a discussion of the health and safety issues as perceived at that point, while in the second part an outline is given of the designer's contribution to the health and safety plan and file, again, as seen at that stage. In five examples the design progresses through three stages (concept, outline and detailed design). In two examples there are four stages, in which the "outline" design stage is expanded into "concept" and "scheme" stages, and in one example, only concept and detailed design stages are used. The number of stages is a matter of convenience and the principles remain the same.

It is not the intention of the Regulations that any "intermediate" stage health and safety plans should exist formally prior to the preparation of the pre-tender stage plan. However, the procedure for the staged development of the plan is one way by which designers can address and clearly document their considerations of hazard and risk in an orderly manner throughout the design process. If significant hazards are not eliminated, they must be taken into account in subsequent design stages. This process eventually leads to the pre-tender stage health and safety plan.

At each design stage, a designer needs to challenge the design assumptions or decisions in the light of the common causes of accidents and ill health. This enables significant hazards to be identified: some of these are subsequently eliminated, while the risks from others are reduced or controlled by adopting the principles of prevention and protection. Some key health and safety issues have been selected in each example and treated in detail to show how risks from hazards can be assessed and reduced. The extended discussion of other hazards has been omitted for reasons of space.

As noted in Sections 1.2 and 2.3, the ACOP makes it clear that the process of risk assessment is an integral part of the design function. Designers have long been aware of the hazards and risks involved in construction and have made assessments in a subjective and qualitative manner. What is new under the 1992 Management of Health and Safety at Work Regulations and the 1994 CDM Regulations is the need for designers formally to weigh health and safety along with other factors and, as appropriate, to analyse and compare the risks associated with different designs. In many ways this represents the nub of the problem for designers and the eight examples illustrate the range of approaches which were adopted in this project. No doubt procedures for assessment of risk by designers will develop and become more refined as experience is gained, but it must be kept in mind that risk assessments are a tool to assist in making better design decisions.

Design development is a process which moves from the general to the particular and a typical development for the bridge example is shown diagramatically in Figure 14. It will be noted that during the preliminary and concept stages, project and element issues are considered and the decisions made affect multiple work sections. Subsequent design stages tend to examine the hazards more on an individual work section basis. Figure 15 contains the elements and work sections based on the CESSM3 classification. Other disciplines will use classifications developed for their particular use (e.g. building services will refer to the NES/CCPI services engineering work sections). This is demonstrated in the bridge example as one way of organising the information required.

## 3.3  STRUCTURE OF EXAMPLES

The structure of the examples reflects the principles set out in Section 3.2 above. The authors of the examples came from different professional backgrounds and so wrote from different perspectives. A common framework is used, but within that the treatments differ in detail. The differences in compilation illustrate the scope for variations in the approaches which may be used by different designers to satisfy the Regulations.

The basic pattern followed in each example is as follows:

1. Introduction - a brief note about whether the project is real or fictitious, the number of design stages used and from which designer's point of view the example has been written.

2. Project information - brief details of the project, location, client etc.

3. Concept study stage - the first part is a discussion of the health and safety issues as identified at the concept study stage, while the second part explains the designer's contributions to the health and safety plan and file at this stage.

4. Outline design stage (in some examples this has been divided into concept and scheme stages) - the first part is again a discussion of health and safety issues identified at the outline design stage, while the second part explains the designer's contribution to the health and safety plan and file at this stage.

5. Detailed design stage - this is normally limited to a discussion of those health and safety issues that have been selected for development during earlier design stages.

6. The health and safety plan for contractor appointment - this is written in the form set out in Appendix 4 of the ACOP. The designer's inputs derived from the example are in bold face, while inputs expected to come from the client, the planning supervisor and other designers are noted in italics.

7. The health and safety file - for brevity, this was limited to a list of heads of the information which the file might contain or reference.

# 4 Refurbishment Project

## 4.1 INTRODUCTION

This example has been prepared from the point of view of an architect in his normal role in a multi-disciplinary design team. It is based on an actual project.

Further explanation [in square brackets] of the thinking behind the notes has been added to aid understanding.

The management of health and safety and the implementation of the CDM Regulations should form part of an integrated approach to design. The aim of this integrated approach is to eliminate the add-on effect by reducing the additional workload to a minimum and to gain spin-off benefits in the design generally.

The tables represent the notes prepared at each design stage by the architect. Were the project to be put on hold with the possibility that the architects who prepared the notes might have no further involvement, the relevant stage report would be enhanced. Similar tables would be produced by the other members of the design team and co-ordinated by the planning supervisor. The tables represent the 'information chain' which is part of the process of continuous design.

Abbreviations used within the text to speed the process are as follows:

- B        Bills of Quantity item
- CM      Construction manager responsibility
- D        No further action, item deleted
- F        Health and safety file item
- P        Health and safety plan item
- PQ      Issue to be raised as part of the contractor's prequalification
- PS      Planning supervisor to confirm action or assumption
- S        Specification item

In this example, the design is progressed through four stages:

- concept
- scheme
- detailed
- tender.

## 4.2 PROJECT INFORMATION

### 4.2.1 Client requirements

The client is a development company, Albion plc. The end user/tenant is the University of Musical Excellence.

The project is to provide 200 student bed sitting rooms in clusters of 4-6 spaces with a bathroom, kitchen/diner and store, if possible, with each cluster. In addition, two studio flats for occasional visitors and a two-bed warden's flat with bath, kitchen and sitting room are to be provided.

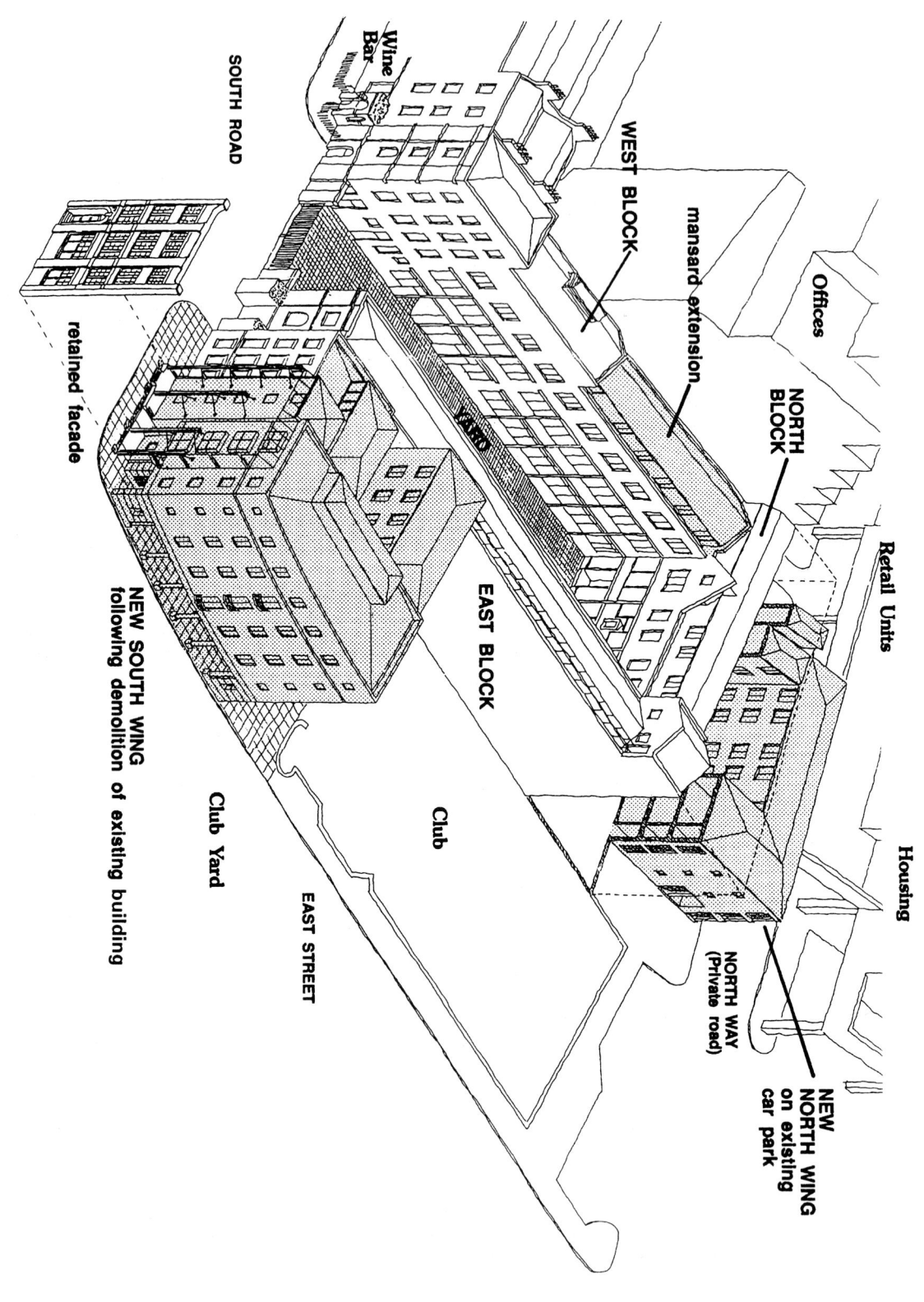

**Figure 1** *Isometric view of the developed design*

### 4.2.2 Description and location

The whole is to be accommodated in a building which was originally part of a Victorian brewery. The most recent use of the building was as offices.

It is envisaged in the brief that two areas will be new build. One portion of new build, the North Wing, will be built in what is now a car park located above a Victorian brick vaulted single storey cellar. The second area of new build, the South Wing, will be located on an area made available by demolishing an existing building.

Additional floor space to be created by adding mansard extensions to the roofs of the East and West Blocks, similar to the mansard on North Block.

Generally, the basement is not used except for a small area for a communal laundry.

The existing building varies in height between three and five storeys, with a single storey basement covering the complete footprint of the site.

The area is of mixed use: residential, office, recreational, etc. It is on the fringe of the City of London in one of the inner boroughs. An isometric view is shown in Figure 1.

### 4.2.3 The design team

The project organisation is complicated and is shown in Figure 2. The contract is JTC'81 Design and Build. The architect is the leader of the design team and reports to the contractor's project manager. For the early part of the project, the project manager undertook the role of planning supervisor. At the start of scheme design a construction manager was appointed who took over the role of planning supervisor (during the construction phase the construction manager would also take on the role of the principle contractor).

A construction management approach is being used to procure the works. Each works contractor is independent with a separate contract with the contractor. The procurement and supervision is undertaken by the construction manager. This complicates the situation regarding the health and safety plan which is a separate and different document for each works contractor. Some parts of the health and safety plan are common to all; some only need slight modification; and some are entirely unique. However, if the health and safety plan was written for a single main contractor, the process and contents would be similar.

### 4.2.4 Local environment

The site is located in a mixed neighbourhood. This has significant impact on the management of health and safety and the contractor's responsibilities for the environment. Some of the types of neighbour are shown on the site plan in Figure 3.

The mix of new build and refurbishment and the problems along the site boundaries are illustrated in Figures 3 and 4.

The case study was written at the end of June 1994 as illustrated in the overall programme in Figure 5. The tender process is about 30% complete. Construction has commenced, with site clearance and demolition almost finished.

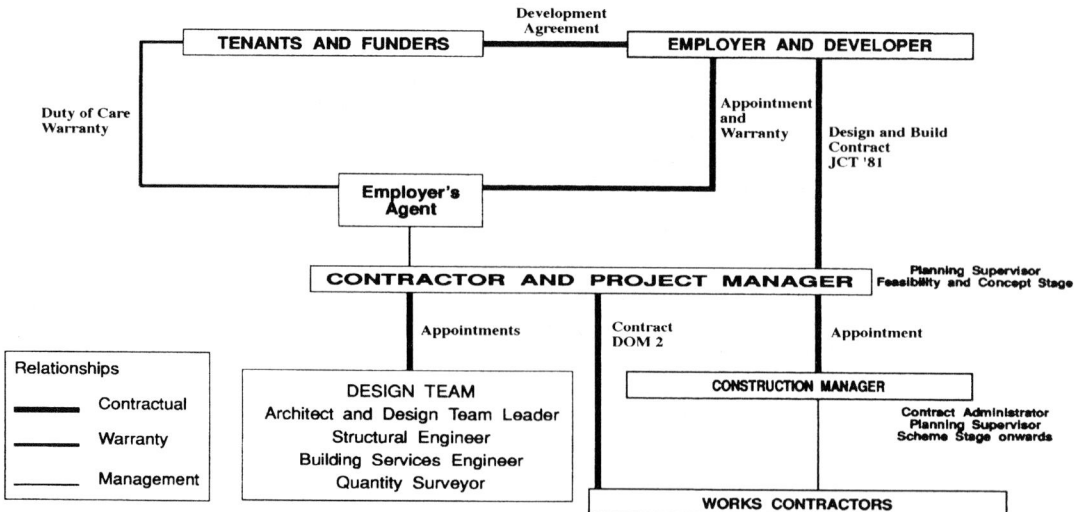

**Figure 2** *Organisation Chart*

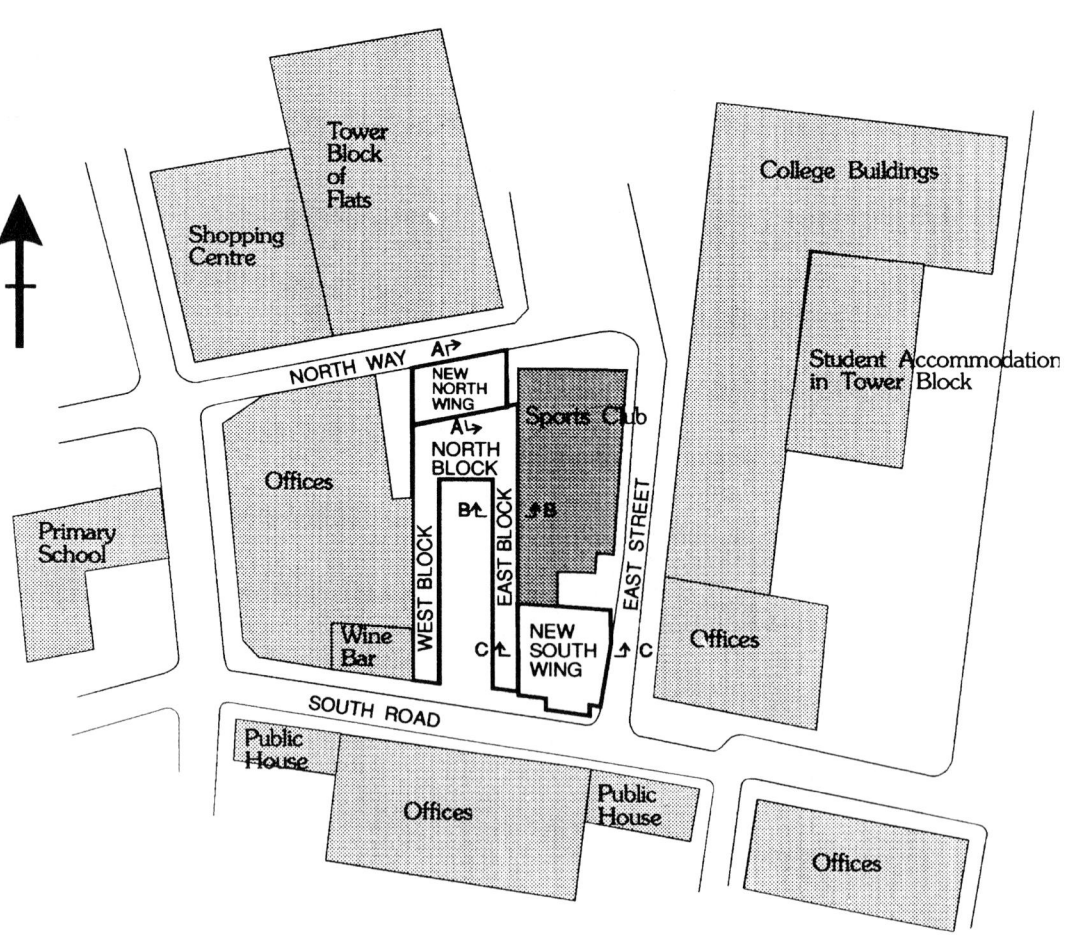

**Figure 3** *Site Plan*

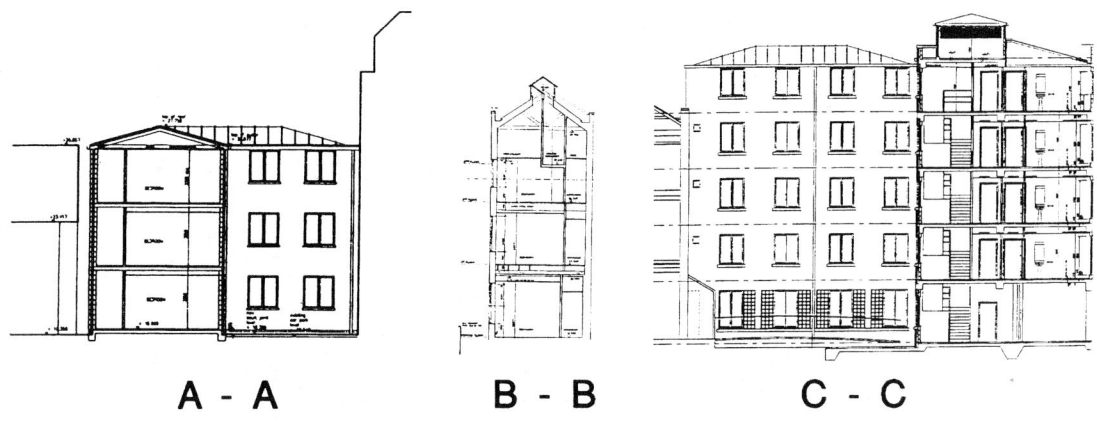

**Figure 4** *General Sections*

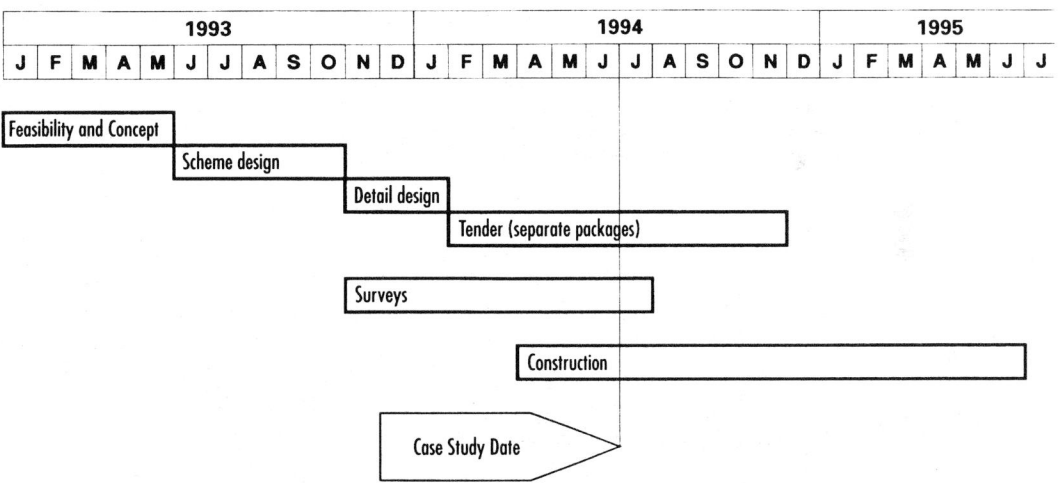

**Figure 5** *Overall Programme*

## 4.3 CONCEPT DESIGN STAGE

Minimal information is available regarding either plan form or integrity of structure, finishes, etc. Work being carried out for developer who was bidding for the site - hence, the need for secrecy.

Outline spec called for 200 bed spaces - little further information available from potential user.

Architect appointed as design team leader; project manager appointed as planning supervisor.

The table below indicates hazards identified and the action taken or to be taken in the future. C/F column identifies those issues which are likely to be included in either the health and safety plan (P) or the health and safety file (F). The notes are deliberately brief. They act as an aide memoire for the final preparation of the health and safety plan and health and safety file. If for any reason the project is suspended, it might be necessary to expand the latest table into a full explanation so that it may be understood by a designer new to the project.

| (a) | Hazard | Action | C/F |
|---|---|---|---|
| 1. | Demolition [Clearly likely to be an action. At this stage all members of the design team recognised the hazard.] | No way to avoid; address detail later. [Action will rest mainly with the structural engineer but no doubt architect will have an option on the solutions investigated to mitigate the risks. It might form part of the H&S File if the demolition were only partial, in which case it would be necessary for the file to demark the new and retained, etc.] | P/F |
| 2. | Existing buildings condition | Survey as soon as permitted. [Design team access very limited so only action is to collect details of survey information which will be required later] | P |
| 3. | No information on services or measured plans, sections, etc. | Survey as soon as permitted | P |
| 4. | Adjacent occupied buildings | No way to avoid; address detail later | P |
| 5. | Multi-storey buildings with single storey basement [Hazard relates to need for scaffolds, possibilities of falling; basement indicates restricted space, etc.] | No way to avoid; address detail later. [Avoidance is the prime aim. In this case it is considered unlikely that the hazard can be avoided; therefore we are looking at ways to minimise the risk globally] | P |
| 6. | Public highways on three sides, private roadway to the rear, narrow one way accesses [Hazards from deliveries, possibly waiting, blocking the narrow roads, etc.] | No way to avoid; address detail later. [A definite element to be addressed in the H&S Plan. Uncertain which member of the design team should comment on such matters, unless there is a highways consultant in the team!] | P |
| 7. | Conservation area and a listed building | No way to avoid; address detail later. [No obvious H&S issues yet but will no doubt have an effect on design so it is worthwhile flagging for future] | P |

| (a) | Hazard | Action | C/F |
|-----|--------|--------|-----|
| 8. | Additional mansard roofs to be added [Formation of structure at high level. Represents an additional hazard to the issues raised by a multi-storey building in 5 above] | No way to avoid; address detail later | P |
| 9. | Possible use of air space over adjacent building [This is a reference to the possibility of adding a further storey height to the Club adjacent. Similar issues to the mansards in 8 above, but an entirely separate set of issues will most probably arise] | Survey as soon as permitted | P |
| 10. | Restricted site, likely to build up to boundaries [Hazards of access, protection of public, working overhand, etc.] | No way to avoid in order to meet brief requirements for capacity; address detail later | P |
| 11. | Deliveries will be difficult during construction [Part of same problem as 6 above but this is how we recorded our thoughts and so it appears as a new item] | No way to avoid; address detail later | P |
| 12. | No information about structural stability but previous use as offices [Use as offices refers to a level of comfort in continuing to plan without survey but with the knowledge that previous use probably required higher floor loading than those our plans will impose] | Survey as soon as permitted | P |
| 13. | Current landlord appears from the external elevations to be maintaining building to above average standard | [Note on hopefully favourable result of surveys just a further comfort really at this stage. Not so much a hazard as the lack of one] | P |
| 14. | Statement from landlord that building contains no asbestos is part of information supplied | Is not a guarantee of non-toxic materials; survey to include c/f [Note to say that this will be checked regardless of the statement. Such statement probably has little standing under H&S legislation unless backed up by survey information, which it is not] | P |

| (b) | Risk Identification | Action taken | C/F |
|-----|---------------------|--------------|-----|
| | No specific assessments at this stage; few issues capable of any real analysis without full surveys. | | P/F |

## 4.4  SCHEME DESIGN STAGE

At this stage the design is developed to the level of detail required to make a planning application.

Initial application to planners resulted in the loss of most of the mansards with only one small area remaining. An area of facade to be demolished will now have to be retained.

To maintain the number of bed spaces, re-design new build to rear using basement area in vaults.

No measured survey information available.

Construction manager (CM) appointed; same organisation is also appointed as planning supervisor, a role previously undertaken by project manager.

Note three additional item types added to C/F column:

- PS      information to planning supervisor
- C       seek confirmation that action will now be responsibility of others
- D       delete from future assessments.

The same hazard reference numbers have been retained throughout so that hazards and risk identification can be tracked uniquely.

| (a) | Hazards | Action | C/F |
|---|---|---|---|
| 1. | Demolition | No change | P |
| 2. | Existing buildings condition | No change | P |
| 3. | No information on services or measured plans, sections, etc. | No change | P |
| 4. | Adjacent occupied buildings | No change | P |
| 5. | Multi-storey buildings | Construction management issue - inform planning supervisor and obtain confirmation [Action: comment is shorthand meaning main problem will addressed by CM as it is more in his field; architect will still have input but CM will lead; planning supervisor to confirm that architect can assume that responsibility for this now rests with CM] | PS<br>C |
| 6. | Public highways on three sides, private roadway to the rear, narrow one way accesses | Construction management issue - inform planning supervisor and obtain confirmation [As issues develop prime responsibility for each hazard will pass to the member of the design team best equipped to assess the risk. The decision as to which member is responsible rests with the planning supervisor] | PS<br>C |
| 7. | Conservation area and a listed building | Design changes have resulted in the reduction of the mansards (Item 8) and the addition of a retained facade (Item 15) | D |

| (a) | Hazards | Action | C/F |
|---|---|---|---|
| 8. | Additional mansard roofs to be added; work at high level | Reduced but still necessary to achieve brief requirements. No way to avoid; address detail later | P |
| 9. | Possible use of air space over adjacent building | Adjacent owner will not permit so no longer a hazard; deleted | D |
| 10. | Restricted site, likely to build up to boundaries | No way to avoid in order to meet brief requirements for capacity. Construction management issue - inform planning supervisor and obtain confirmation | PS C |
| 11. | Deliveries will be difficult during construction | Construction management issue - inform planning supervisor and obtain confirmation | PS C |
| 12. | No information about structural stability, but previous use as offices | No change | P |
| 13. | [only a note at concept design stage has since been omitted] | Deleted | D |
| 14. | Asbestos and other toxic materials | Survey as soon as permitted | P |
| 15. | Basement construction cutting through existing Victorian brick, concrete, etc. [Hazards such as noise, vibration, brick dust, structural support to vaults, etc.] | No way to avoid as is necessary for disabled access; add to list of surveys; address detail later | P |
| 16. | Ventilation to basement vault area in construction, access/ egress confinement, etc. [Separate issue to the cutting above and an extension to item 5] | Construction management issue - inform planning supervisor and obtain confirmation | PS C |
| 17. | Retained facade [Hazards similar to demolition but now likely to involve architect to a greater extent in defining which elements to retain; discussions with engineer regarding temporary supports and effect on final design] | Discuss design options with structural engineer and rest of design team [Extension to item 1 above] | |
| 18. | Archaeology, burials possible, high degree of organic preservation likely [Organic preservation could indicate contaminated land] | Information obtained from archaeologists. Possible need to investigate for soil contamination. | P |

| (a) | Hazards | Action | C/F |
|---|---|---|---|
| 19. | Removal/cutting existing walls [Hazards related to items 1 and 15; possibility of local collapse and/or major frame weakening] | Establish structure from survey; structural engineer and CM possibly more involved | P |

| (b) | Risk Identification | Action taken | C/F |
|---|---|---|---|
| 18. | Archaeology, burials possible, high degree of organic preservation likely | Risk is only slight, but effect could be serious. Discussed with rest of team - use of bored piles rather than strip footings will reduce exposure and total volume excavated. Risk reduced but not eliminated. Borehole survey to include test for human remains | P |
| 19. | Removal/cutting existing walls | Survey walls to determine if structural. Structural engineering issue - inform planning supervisor and obtain confirmation. Keep cutting into existing structure to a minimum | PS C |

Potential hazards merely identified at this stage. Further information to be gathered before risk may be assessed.

## 4.5  DETAILED DESIGN STAGE

Developer released funds and building owner issued licence to enter premises and make physical investigations.

Full measured survey undertaken.

Infestation survey reveals no current problem. [A timber consultant was briefed rather than a representative from a chemical company.]

Areas opened to reveal structure, nature of finishes, condition of built-in services.

Local surveys of minor elements as required by designers undertaken on site by CM staff.

Drawings obtained from previous owner, owner's consultants, previous consultants - all show inconsistencies so very little practical use.

Brief changed:

• ratio of beds to kitchens, etc. reduced
• no windows overlooking Club yard
• escape into Club yard not permitted.

Boundary line established. Boundary on north side at ground level not aligned with structure of basement vaults. Boundary line passes part way through an arch!

Additional item type added to C/F column:

• CM        construction management issue

| (a) | Hazards | Action | C/F |
|-----|---------|--------|-----|
| 1. | Demolition | No way to avoid; address detail in tender documents | P |
| 2. | Existing buildings condition | Survey completed - issues arising:<br>• Warren truss in North block first floor<br>• Raised floor fixed and not removable in North block<br>• Parapet insecure on retained facade | P |
| 3. | No information on services or measured plans, sections, etc. | Surveys completed; hazards resulting dealt with separately under new heads. Delete item | D |
| 4. | Adjacent occupied buildings | No change | P |
| 5. | Multi-storey buildings | Deleted | D |
| 6. | Public highways on three sides | Deleted | D |
| 7. | Conservation area, etc. | Deleted | D |
| 8. | Additional mansard roofs to be added; work at high level | Reduced but still necessary to achieve brief requirements. No way to avoid; address detail in tender documents | P |
| 9. | Possible use of air space | Deleted | D |
| 10. | Restricted site | Deleted | D |
| 11. | Deliveries will be difficult | Deleted | D |
| 12. | Information about structural stability | Survey completed. Structural engineering issue - inform planning supervisor and obtain confirmation | PS<br>C |
| 13. | Current maintenance standards | Deleted | D |
| 14. | Asbestos and other toxic materials | Survey required | P |
| 15. | Basement construction cutting through existing Victorian brick, concrete, etc. | No way to avoid as necessary for disabled access; add to list of surveys; address detail later | P |
| 16. | Ventilation to basement vault area | Deleted | D |
| 17. | Retained facade | Mainly a structural engineering issue - inform planning supervisor and obtain confirmation | PS<br>C |
| 18. | Archaeology, burials possible, high degree of organic preservation likely | Boreholes reveal no abnormal organic matter. Trial holes in basements reveal only likely place is new build area to south, area to north built on virgin ground. Address later | P |

| (a) | Hazards | Action | C/F |
|-----|---------|--------|-----|
| 19. | Removal/cutting existing walls | No way to avoid at least some; address as it develops with structural engineer and construction manager | P |
| 20. | Design team access into unoccupied buildings, including basement areas. [Hazard confined space for working] | Issue instructions regarding access rules. Entry controlled by construction manager | CM |
| 21. | Means of escape from fire during construction | Generally current buildings have safe means of escape. Contractors should have no problems provided means of escape remain operational. Controlled during construction by construction manager. Confirm with planning supervisor | P<br>PS<br>CM |
| 22. | Survey of drains designed for brewery operations and flow | Services engineer issue - inform planning supervisor and obtain confirmation | PS<br>C |
| 23. | Building up to boundaries and over footpath as previous building. Window cleaning problem overcome by making all windows turn for cleaning from inside, except ground floor where additional security required and the yard where safety devices are already fixed | Construction manager obtained approval to close footpath to public during construction. Construction management issue - inform planning supervisor and obtain confirmation. Check yard safety devices are secure and in good order; if not arrange replacement | PS<br>C<br><br><br>CM |
| 24. | Building adjacent to conservatory of neighbouring Club, operation of which vital to Club. | Design temporary dust and sound barrier to be installed before any works commence adjacent to Club. Construction management issue - inform planning supervisor and obtain confirmation | PS<br>C |
| 25. | Compactors at rear, one to remove, one to remain in place | After one compactor has been removed, spillage is noticeable. CM to arrange to clean area. Remaining container responsibility of adjacent building occupier. Construction management issue; inform planning supervisor and obtain confirmation | PS<br>C |
| 26. | Raised floor fixed and not removable in North block, extension of item 2 [May not be a hazard in the long term. The floors which were believed to be removable are in fact fixed by loose tongues which have been glued in place] | Remove section of floor to investigate construction and condition of floor, subfloor condition and service routes. Address detail later | P |

| 27. | Parapet insecure on retained facade - extension of item 2 | Structural engineering issue - inform planning supervisor and obtain confirmation [Only necessary to remove and rebuild if structural engineer determines that brickwork is insecure upon close inspection, otherwise retain] | PS<br>C |
|---|---|---|---|

| (b) | **Risk Identification** | **Action taken** | **C/F** |
|---|---|---|---|
| 1. | Demolition and retained facade | Structural engineer to inform contractor of structural survey results. No obvious signs of asbestos, survey undertaken, none found. Risk considered normal for competent demolition contractor. The site is adjacent to the public highway on two sides and good means of escape are available. Construction manager to prequalify contractors on this basis. Construction management issue - inform planning supervisor and obtain confirmation | PS<br>C<br>CM |
| 2. | Warren truss in North block first floor | Access through Warren truss possible without any structural modification, by lowering raised floor to obtain minimum width and height of corridor. Hazard eliminated | D |
| 8. | Additional mansard roofs to be added; work at high level | Design to maximise off-site pre-fabrication and minimise period installers at risk on roof construction. Fall only possible east side, west protected by adjacent building at higher level. Note danger of damage, security, etc. to adjacent occupied building. Risk considered normal for competent steel frame and roofing contractors. Construction manager to prequalify contractors on this basis. Construction management issue - inform planning supervisor and obtain confirmation | PS<br>C<br>CM |
| 15. | Basement construction cutting through existing Victorian brick, concrete, etc. | In conjunction with structural engineer and construction manager, consider methods of structural support of existing brick arches and cutting methods to minimise noise and dust to operatives and neighbours | P |
| 19. | Removal/cutting existing walls | In each case ask construction manager to investigate existing structure with structural engineer to obtain precise situation before design issued for construction | P |
| 20. | Design team access into unoccupied buildings | Building was occupied until recently. All holes cut by construction manager have been covered or filled. All services are cut off. Main problem is lack of light and danger of being trapped by 'normal' accident and inability to call for help. Design team to be warned of danger. Architects to be issued with reminder to consult Office Safety Manual on measures to be taken [torches, mobile phone, joint visiting arrangements, etc.] | CM |

## 4.6 TENDER STAGE

At tender stage each package of work is considered separately. The whole project is now split into packages for management and administration.

Further letters added to C/F column:

- B      to be included in Bills of Quantity
- PQ     issue to be raised during prequalification
- QS     issue to be raised with quantity surveyor
- S      to be included in specification.

### 4.6.1   Demolition package

In prequalifying this package, the demolition contractor should demonstrate facade retention experience and, either have in-house designers, or regularly use external designers for the retention system design. The designer of the retention system must also carry his own professional indemnity insurance (PI) which should be no less than £500,000 per occurrence.

| (a) | Hazards | Action | C/F |
|---|---|---|---|
| 1. | Demolition and retained facade | Structural engineer has suggested that:<br><br>• basement is filled to increase stability<br>• part of permanent structure is used to provide partial temporary support.<br><br>Design to be provided to tenderers assessed by structural engineer for stability and architect for conformity to permanent design | P |
| 5. | Multi-storey building and single storey basement | Deleted | D |
| 14. | Asbestos | Survey undertaken, none found | P<br>F |
| 18. | Archaeology, burials possible, high degree of organic preservation likely | Boreholes reveal no abnormal organic matter. Trial holes in basements reveal only likely place is new build area to south, area to north built on virgin ground. Inform tenderers of information | P<br>F |
| 24. | Building adjacent to conservatory of neighbouring Club, operation of which vital to Club | Details of dust and sound temporary barrier form part of tender documents. Instruction in tender that barrier to be installed before any works commenced adjacent to Club | P |
| 28. | Statutory services | All building services cut off at boundary by enabling works contractor. Statutory undertakers plans provided to tenderers. Building services engineer issue | P |

| (a) | Hazards | Action | C/F |
|---|---|---|---|
| 29. | Survey information | Parapet insecure on retained facade. Inform tenderers and bill as a repair as part of works. Part of structure has wooden floors; include note to this effect. Also provide tenderers with available as-built drawings, suitably annotated for the current situation, dimensional survey and photographs. Insist on site visit to inspect trial pits in basement and trial holes through walls, beams, etc. | P |
| 30. | Adjacent occupied buildings | No way to avoid; address detail in tender documents | P |
| 31. | Information about structural stability | Survey completed; structural engineering issue | P |
| 32. | Demolition over footpath | Construction manager obtained approval to close footpath to public during construction | P |

| (b) | Risk Identification | Action taken | C/F |
|---|---|---|---|
| 1. | Demolition and retained facade | Normal risk for competent demolition contractor. Check status and PI of temporary works designer | |
| 5. | Multi-storey building with single basement | Deleted | D |
| 14. | Asbestos | Survey undertaken, none found | P F |
| 18. | Archaeology, burials possible, high degree of organic preservation likely | No change | P F |
| 24. | Building adjacent to conservatory of neighbouring Club, operation of which vital to Club | Details of dust and sound temporary barrier form part of tender documents. Instruction in tender that barrier is to be installed before any works commenced adjacent to Club | P |
| 28. | Statutory services | Note incomplete information available. Construction manager to arrange hand dug trial pits to determine location in footpath to East Street | P F |
| 29. | Survey information | Parapet insecure on retained facade. Inform tenderers and bill as a repair as part of works. Part of structure has wooden floors; include note to this effect. Also provide tenderers with available as-built drawings, suitably annotated for the current situation, dimensional survey and photographs. Insist on site visit to inspect trial pits in basement and trial holes through walls, beams, etc. | P |

| (b) **Risk Identification** | **Action taken** | **C/F** |
|---|---|---|
| 30. Adjacent occupied buildings | No way to avoid; address detail in tender documents | P |
| 31. Information about structural stability | Survey completed; structural engineering issue | P |
| 32. Demolition over footpath | Construction manager obtained approval to close footpath to public during construction | P |

### 4.6.2　Brick and block package

The analysis below has resulted in the decision to appoint a specialist glass block installer, and hence this package is normal brick and block for the purposes of prequalification.

| (a) **Hazards** | **Action** | **C/F** |
|---|---|---|
| 14. Asbestos | Survey undertaken, none found | P<br>F |
| 15. Basement construction cutting through existing Victorian brick, concrete, etc. | Noise and dust hazards - acceptable? Occupied housing adjacent - working hours restrictions even after all normal noise controls and equipment used? Possibility of discovering construction not as expected. Price risk for QS to allow in tender docs. | P<br>B |
| 19. Removal/cutting existing walls | What is extent and type of structure to be cut? | P |
| 24. Building adjacent to conservatory of neighbouring Club, operation of which vital to Club | Dust and sound temporary barrier to be installed by demolition contractor as part of his works. Is this adequate for this element of the works? | P |
| 30. Adjacent occupied buildings | Overhand working may be required | P |
| 33. Structural safety | Check if all lintels specified are standard [i.e. all lintels are for standard BS openings, otherwise structural engineer may have to design and/or check contractor's proposals] | P |
| 34. Size and weight of blocks | Investigate size and weight of blocks | P |
| 35. Use of glass blocks | Relatively common item, but worth looking at specific hazards | P<br>B |
| 36. Permanent windows to be built in with masonry. Free issue of joinery to brick and block contractor | Is risk increased or reduced overall by this productivity requirement? | P |

| (a) | Hazards | Action | C/F |
|-----|---------|--------|-----|
| 37. | Roof fixed on front new build in advance of lower levels of masonry. Roof supported off top storey height of masonry rather than off steel frame. Internal walls also masonry to provide additional stability. | Brick and block contractor to lay top storey first. Programme requirement. Main hazard is fixing of roof over brick and block contractor working below [Unusual requirement in programme terms, does have an impact on the contractor's approach to the safety of operatives whilst the roof is being installed at a level above] | P |
| 38. | Rendered finish to be painted | Is there any better solution to paint as a finish, given the difficult access now and for future maintenance? | P |
| 39. | Deliveries will be difficult as scaffolds will be on highway | Are there any less hazardous alternatives? | P |

| (b) | Risk Identification | Action taken | C/F |
|-----|---------------------|--------------|-----|
| 15. | Basement construction cutting through existing Victorian brick, concrete, etc. | Diamond stitch drilling considered a safe and the least environmentally damaging method of cutting existing brick [Slow, but use of water and drill action produces almost no noise or dust. Additionally, action in cutting brick does not cause any distress to adjacent brickwork]. Invite tenderers to propose alternatives to diamond stitch drilling specified to reduce cost but maintaining safety aspects | P B |
| 19. | Removal/cutting existing walls | Very little required; all areas have been investigated by enabling gang. Little risk of unexpected discoveries. Design of temporary supports not a problem as designed at present. Minimal risk beyond that normally to be expected by experienced contractor. Mention survey work already done | P |
| 24. | Building adjacent to conservatory of neighbouring Club, operation of which vital to Club | Dust and sound temporary barrier installed by demolition contractor as part of his works considered adequate protection also for these works. Leave in place to protect brick and block works. Brick and block contractor to remove once permanent wall in place. Will have to remove out of normal Club hours to protect members. Note to quantity surveyor regarding requirement for out-of-hours working | P B QS |
| 30. | Adjacent occupied buildings | Overhand working is only way some elements can be constructed. Should not form high risk if properly planned and scaffold designed to accommodate | P |

| (b) | Risk Identification | Action taken | C/F |
|---|---|---|---|
| 33. | Structural safety, lintels | All are standard. Normal risk for contractor - will only mention fact that all lintels are standard in plan to stop tenderers looking for specials | P |
| 34. | Size and weight of blocks | Managed to reduce to two sizes: 100 and 140. Maximum strength specified is 10N. Should be handleable with ease. Maximum size and weights proposed is acceptable for single hand laying | D |
| 35. | Use of glass blocks | Talks with normal brick and block contractors under consideration indicate they are keen to do this work but cannot guarantee experienced operatives. Therefore, employ specialist to install. Ensure at prequalification that firm is specialist and has necessary experience. If so, not a hazard | PQ |
| 36. | Permanent windows to be built-in with masonry. Free issue of joinery to brick and block contractor | Overall site hazard reduced if glazed at factory but increased risk to brick and block contractor [Increased risk due to presence of glass whilst handling and fixing. Still less hazardous than fixing glass at site at heights, in winds, etc.] Risk to brick and block contractor high but not unacceptable, given the alternatives. Instructions regarding handling to be included in plan. Tenderers must give method statement in tender to prove experience | P<br>B |
| 37. | Roof installed to front new build in advance of lower levels of masonry. Roof supported off top storey height of masonry, rather than off steel frame. Internal walls also masonry to provide additional stability, agreed with structural engineer | Brick and block contractor working below roofer is far less than ideal. Alternative is unacceptable in programme terms. Hence, take precautions. Must be vertical separation. Construction manager to organise construction phases to allow for vertical separation. Tenderers method statement to include specific mention of this item | P<br>B |
| 38. | Rendered finish to be painted | Alternative of self-coloured render not acceptable as colour deteriorates, producing an unacceptable finish in a short period. [Alternative of not rendering wall not possible due to planning requirement.] Paint with long durability required. Product in mind, but include as performance spec. [Performance spec preferable to product since contractor may know of less hazardous material which satisfies spec.] Performance spec. to include statement on material hazard of paint | P<br>S |

| (b) | Risk Identification | Action taken | C/F |
|-----|---------------------|--------------|-----|
| 39. | Deliveries will be difficult as scaffolds will be on highway | Risk not high provided rules on loading out scaffold stages are observed. Note in plan and to construction manager as principal contractor to pay particular attention to stage loading. Control of deliveries to form part of tenderers' method statement, looking for a just-in-time solution consistent with reliable supply | P |

## 4.7 THE ARCHITECT'S CONTRIBUTION TO THE PRE-TENDER STAGE HEALTH AND SAFETY PLAN*

### 1. Introduction

The works are being tendered under a construction management form using the JCT'81 subcontract form, DOM2. The construction manager is appointed as both the planning supervisor and the principal contractor. Each subcontract represents a 'package' of work, usually on a trade basis, but often including additions which either reduce conflict between packages or make the package more commercially attractive. In addition, the prequalification of works contractors has been tailored in respect of the planning supervisor's expectations regarding the 'normal' level of competency. This is particularly important if health and safety plans are to be produced at tender stage which contribute in a positive manner to health and safety management by clarifying those features which are abnormal or which the tenderer would normally have to investigate. A standard list of 'normal' health and safety factors would merely serve to confuse the 'real' issues.

The following sections are common to all 'packages':

• Nature of project
• Existing environment
• Existing drawings
• Site wide elements
• Overlap with client
• Site rules.

The following sections are written specifically for each 'package':

• Design
• Construction materials
• Continuing liaison.

Examples of two specific packages are included:

• Demolition
• Brick and blockwork.

* In this example plan, the case study designer's inputs to the plan are shown in bold face, while the inputs of others are shown in italics.

## 2.    Nature of project

[Should be written by the planning supervisor, although the architect would be an obvious choice to prepare a draft for the planning supervisor to incorporate into the health and safety plan]

Name of client:          *Albion plc*

Location:                *Inner London borough*

The construction work:   *The project is for the conversion of parts of a Victorian brewery, whose last use was as offices, into student accommodation. The accommodation is arranged with three to five study/bedrooms sharing a kitchen/diner, bathroom, toilet and store. Each bedroom has a handbasin. Special conditions apply to the room-to-room sound attenuation as the students are studying music and will be practising in their rooms. The only common facility is a laundry to be provided in the existing basement. The remaining areas of the basement will be for temporary accommodation only during these works. The basement may be converted to other common uses following completion of these works.*

*Although generally a conversion, there are three areas of new build:*

- *a new North Wing*
- *a new South Wing*
- *and a small length of mansard over the West Block.*

*The building is to be fully fitted, including all loose furniture, etc.*

Timescale for completion
of construction work:     *Construction will commence in May 1994 and all works will be complete by the end of June 1995.*

*The works will be procured in a series of works packages by a construction manager who will also be the contract administrator and principle contractor. Each works contractor will have a separate contract with the design and build contractor.*

## 3.    Existing environment

[Similar comments to above regarding drafting]

*The area is of mixed use with domestic housing, student accommodation, a school, public houses, a wine bar, a fitness club, offices, a supermarket and a shopping precinct all within close proximity. The shopping precinct and supermarket have recently begun to trade for seven days a week.*

*The roads are generally narrow. The main access is the South Road which is two-way and gives access to the Yard. Roads to the east and west are one-way as is the private road to the north.*

*The surrounding buildings are also relatively tall and hence noise will be transmitted to them where it would in more normal circumstances be dissipated.*

*The building is leased and the freeholder has his corporate head office on the south side of South Road, immediately opposite the gates to the Yard.*

*The Environmental Health Officer has served a Section 60 notice (under the Control of Pollution Act 1974) on the site. A copy is included in the tender documents.*

*The ground is generally Victorian fills about 3m deep overlying Thames gravels. Within the Victorian fills there is a slight chance of discovering human burials from the Roman period. No excavation is envisaged which would affect the burial areas.* [ May need to place stronger emphasis on this point for the piling package.]

## 4.     Existing drawings

**There are no drawings of existing structure or services which have been found to be reliable. Any information from such drawings which may be in the possession of the contractor is to be submitted to the construction manager prior to use.**

## 5.     The design

(a) Demolition package

*The structural engineer has designed the permanent frame to be used as part of the temporary support system. The balance of the design (i.e. the temporary elements) is to be provided by the demolition contractor. The demarcation is defined on the drawings provided.*

(b) Brick and blockwork package

**There are areas of glass blocks shown on the drawings. These form part of a separate package and are not part of these works.**

## 6.     Construction materials

(a) Demolition package

[*Steel and paint finish to be specified by the structural engineer. Colour not important at this stage as all permanent steel will be repainted.*]

(b) Brick and blockwork package

**The materials are as normally expected. The maximum size and weight of block is 140 by 10N. Glass blocks are used quite extensively. There is also painted render for which a performance spec is given, including durability, frequency of cleaning and repainting. It is thought that none of the self-coloured mortars has the required ability to weather well. The paint proposed must take account of toxicity and the precautions required.**

## 7.     Site wide elements

[This section would be provided by the construction manager in this instance. For more conventional design teams, the architect may be the most appropriate member of the design team to draft this section.]

*Access to the site will generally be via the main gates in South Road to the Yard. Access to the new North and South wings will usually be from the roads for immediate deliveries. Once the frames are complete, access for operatives and materials will be from the converted areas of the building.*

*For the fitting out phases, a common user hoist should be provided giving access to all levels from the north east corner of the Yard.*

*Given that all common user welfare facilities (canteen, toilets, drying room) are located in the basement below the Yard, a risk assessment will have been undertaken by the contractor/planning supervisor. Sub-contractors will have space allocated in the Yard for a temporary office and some storage. Water for the works will be free. Power for the works will be free and supplied at 110v from 25kva transformers at suitable locations.*

*Power for the offices will be submetered.*

*There will be no parking of cars nor commercial vehicles unless collecting or delivering goods or tools.*

*The roads adjacent to the site are part of an area parking system and waiting will not be permitted. Transit mixers and vehicles carrying like materials must be in radio contact with the site so that they can be called from parking areas close to, but not on, the site.*

## 8.      Overlap with client

**There are no specific rules related to any client activities.**

## 9.      Site Rules

[Similar comment on authorship to Site wide elements]

*There will be no smoking on the site.*

*No noisy work as defined in the attached Section 60 notice will be permitted between the hours stated.*

*Tenderers' attention is drawn to the construction manager's requirements provided in the tender documents at Section 3. These must be fully taken into account at time of tender.*

## 10.     Continuing liaison

(a) Demolition package

**The contractor is to submit final drawings and full calculations for the temporary works to the construction manager at least five working days before fabrication is due to commence.** [*The CM will arrange to distribute to the design team and give final approval. In this respect the CM is acting in his capacity as planning supervisor and contract administrator. The architect's interest will be in ensuring that none of the temporary works obstructs the installation of permanent works as the design is sequentially completed.*]

## 4.8   THE HEALTH AND SAFETY FILE

In the same manner that the health and safety plan above only presents fully the architect's contribution, this section only details the architect's contribution to the health and safety file. The structural engineer would provide all structural drawings and design loadings; the construction manager would provide a method statement of the construction sequence; the services engineer would provide the design parameters; the services contractor would provide as built drawings of all services and public utility systems together with operation and maintenance manuals etc. This is not an exhaustive list, but is included to illustrate the variety of sources from which the planning supervisor would draw to present the final file to the client.

The architect would prepare:

- A précis of the brief
- General arrangement drawings including details of fire compartmentalisation, fire protected routes, etc.
- A schedule of all materials used together with colour and catalogue references
- Methods of window cleaning
- Methods of maintaining other non-standard systems, for example the north wall of the new South Wing.

This is not a definitive list since the project has not yet reached this stage. It reflects current opinion on what eventually will be produced.

# 5   New build project

## 5.1   INTRODUCTION

This case study is for a small new build project of six two-bedroom flats typical of those undertaken by small architectural practices. It is based on a real project.

This example of the design development is written from the point of view of the architect designer only, another person being appointed as the planning supervisor.

The design is progressed in four stages:

- concept
- outline
- scheme
- detailed.

'F' in the right-hand margin denotes an item which should be incorporated in the project file and 'P' an item to be included in the health and safety plan.

## 5.2   PROJECT INFORMATION

### 5.2.1   Location

The site is located on a triangular plot, as shown on the site plan (Figure 6), adjacent to a main railway line on an embankment and a busy local road.

The site was previously owned by British Rail and contained an Electricity Board substation which has been removed.                                                                                        P/F

### 5.2.2   Client requirements

The client is a housing association and the brief is to construct six two-bedroom flats of not less than 61 sq m.

The budget for the project is £200,000 and the flats are to be completed in six months after possession of the site.

## 5.3   CONCEPT DESIGN STAGE

### 5.3.1   Discussion of health and safety issues

*Railway line*

As part of the sale particulars, a 2m high chain line fence is to be constructed and maintained by

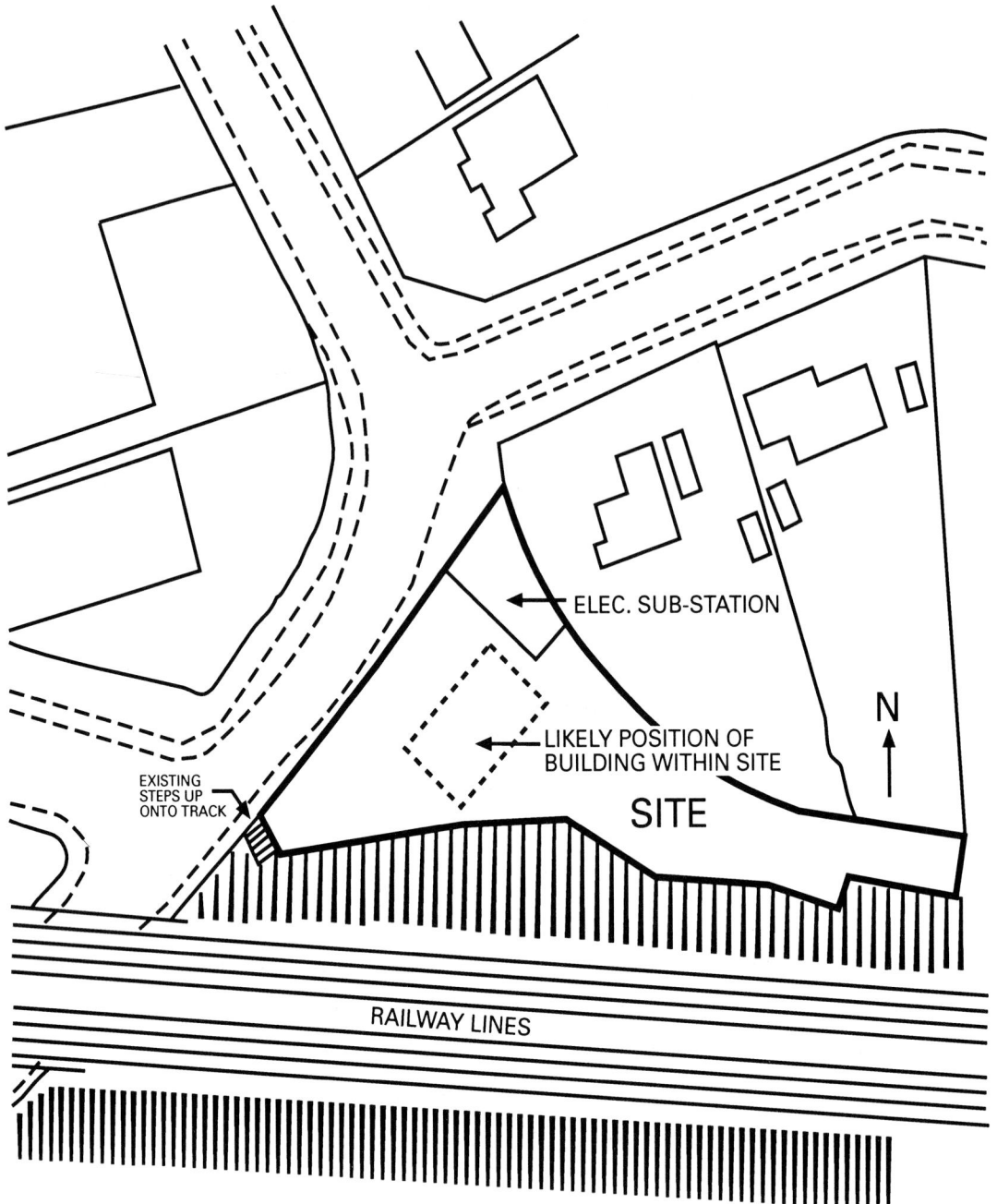

**Figure 6** *Site plan*

the developer to a line set out by British Rail. The existing access steps by the bridge are to be retained.

P

The principal contractor, however, will need to erect a temporary fence during construction in order to prevent unauthorised access.

P

Discussions with Railtrack confirmed they did not consider that the development would affect the operation and maintenance of the railway line.

P/F

It was also confirmed that the relative distances and levels between the development and the electrified track were such that no earthing of scaffolding would be required.

P/F

Further details of any cranes used during construction were to be submitted.

The principal contractor is to submit details of any crane he proposes to use for Railtrack approval.   P

### Electricity substation

The remaining concrete slab and gravelled areas are heavily soiled with oil.   P/F

Although this is not considered to be of great importance, the client is advised to appoint a specialist to report on this matter and to make recommendations as to its treatment or removal.

Specialist report to be obtained for inclusion in project file and safety plan.   P/F

### Access road

The access road is a very busy local road throughout the day.

The site is on a bend in the road which, coupled with the railway bridge abutments, hinders visibility.

Delivery of materials will be difficult because:

- parking in the road to off-load will cause a definite hazard to road users and should be avoided   P

- entering and leaving the site must be strictly controlled by the principal contractor if accidents are to be avoided.   P

The  principal contractor must state how he will deal with this matter at tender submission in the method statement.   P

The preferred contractor will be required to provide method statements prior to the post tender examination.

### Services

All main services are available and easily accessed for construction, except for the foul sewer which is in the centre of the road and is six metres deep.   P/F

The principal contractor is to incorporate his health and safety measures in his method statement at tender stage.   P

Investigations have indicated that there are no other underground or overhead services on the site.   F

### Rights Of Way

There are no public rights of way.   P

## 5.3.2   Designer's contribution to health and safety plan and file

Both the plan and file are opened and the relevant information placed as noted above.

## 5.4. OUTLINE DESIGN STAGE

### 5.4.1    Discussion of health and safety issues

Due to the characteristics of the site, any building will be parallel to the road frontage and occupy as much of it as possible as the site narrows to the rear.  In order to accommodate the six flats the building is likely to be three storeys in height.

As a result, once construction reaches first floor level, vehicular access to the rear will be under the upper floors of the building.

*Issues*

* some delivery vehicles may be prohibited in accessing rear part of site

* tall vehicles over three metres, such as furniture vans, will only have access to the front of building

* sufficient forecourt to be provided to allow adequate space for tall vehicles to park temporarily and to turn and exit in a forward direction, as there will not be sufficient room to include a lay-by

* sight lines, especially from the bridge, to be carefully established in order to position cross-over                                                                                            P

* effort to be made to site building as far away as possible from the railway embankment

* in order to maintain low ridge height towards the adjoining house, the top floor is to be within roof space with either dormer window or roof lights, which in both cases can be cleaned from the inside.                                                                      P/F

### 5.4.2    Designer's contribution to health and safety plan and file

Both plan and file to be amplified with identified items.

## 5.5    SCHEME DESIGN STAGE

### 5.5.1    Discussion of health and safety issues

Building to be of conventional load bearing wall on strip foundations and precast concrete floor construction, including a suspended ground floor and pitched roof with roof lights and dormer windows.

Design consideration of construction materials:

* bricks               Standard - no risk.

* blocks               Majority of blockwork 100mm but some 150mm may be required.

| | | |
|---|---|---|
| • pc floors | Comparison made between pc slab or beam and pot. Beam and pot chosen for the following reasons: <br> - lighter and smaller components <br> - easier to provide service holes <br> - easier delivery and positioning avoiding large cranes on <br>    cramped site. | P/F |
| | Layout of beams and pots to be recorded. | P/F |
| • dry lining | All walls and underside of floor slabs drylined with plasterboard on battens for the following reasons: <br> - less wet trade <br> - easier distribution of services in voids. Note that services will <br>    be concealed behind plasterboard. | P/F |
| • floor finishes | Choice between dry floating floor and 75mm sand and cement screed and sound insulating quilt discussed in order to avoid mechanical preparation of top of slab. Sand and cement screed chosen on cost grounds. | P/F |
| | Layout of beam/pot to be recorded at detailed design stage. | P/F |
| • windows | All windows to be fixed from inside and glazing to be fixed with internal beads. | |
| | This decision will involve an extra cost initially but will be safer to maintain and replace. It also provides better security. | F |
| | All windows capable of being cleaned from inside. | F |
| | All windows to be double glazed to reduce the noise from the railway. | |
| • paints | All paints to be water-based. | F |
| • roofs | It was appreciated that sloping roofs could constitute a risk, particularly for maintenance. | |
| | However, to satisfy planning requirements, the roofs would be pitched and no extra supports or fixing plates would be provided as they might cause maintenance problems during the life of the building. | |
| | It was also considered that any roof maintenance would be carried out by a competent contractor and a layman would be unlikely to attempt to access or maintain the roof slopes. | P |
| • TV aerials | Note that they are to be fixed to gable ends only, or within roof space if possible. | P/F |
| • drainage | Note that last manhole before sewer connection will be a deep excavation. To be considered further at detailed design stage. | P/F |

### 5.5.2  Designer's contribution to the health and safety plan and file

Both the plan and file are developed to include the relevant items identified in the scheme design stage.

## 5.6 DETAILED DESIGN STAGE

### 5.6.1 Discussion of health and safety issues

Detailed design consideration continues on basis established at the previous stage.

Structural engineer confirms structural elements previously considered.

Soil investigation of electricity substation indicates that contamination is not significant.

Elements of substation have to be removed to form new hardstanding area for car parking and turning space.

### *Services*

Position of all radiators considered to prevent them becoming a hazard, e.g. on a staircase landing.

Position of all power points and lighting points carefully considered both for functional use and to prevent possible hazards, e.g. ceiling points above staircase.

Position of individual cold/hot water storage units considered and detailed in order to
facilitate maintenance, access for controls, and ability to drain down easily.                    F

### *Fire precaution*

Consider means of escape and consult with Building Control on all aspects within
this section.  Include fire plan in file.                                                        P/F

### *Drainage*

The position of invert level of last manhole within the site is established.  This will be five metres deep.  Consideration is given as to whether contractor should construct connection from last manhole to sewer, or whether to subcontract this to Local Authority.

It is decided that the contractor will construct last manhole, but drain run and connection will be subcontracted to Local Authority.

### *General construction*

The resulting design is for a three storey building with a pitched roof which could be constructed by a competent small/middle-sized builder using conventional scaffolding and limited cranage/ hoisting equipment.

### *External works*

Ensure and check correct position of setting of pavement cross-over as this is crucial in
providing current sight lines.  This must be agreed with the highway authority.                  P/F

Consider external lighting to identify obstacles at night and to provide security.

Landscaping - carefully consider positioning and size of planting to prevent a hazard by obscuring vision or providing areas for concealment.

## 5.7 THE ARCHITECT'S CONTRIBUTION TO THE PRE-TENDER STAGE HEALTH AND SAFETY PLAN*

### 1. General

*All prospective tenderers (principal contractor) will receive a health and safety plan. The purpose is to identify the main health and safety issues regarding the construction work and form the basis for tenderers to submit their proposals for managing the problems.*

*The successful principal contractor will develop this health and safety plan as part of his duties.*

### 2. Nature of project

| | |
|---|---|
| Name of client: | **A Housing Association** |
| Location: | **An urban location one mile from city centre.** |
| The construction work: | **The construction of six two-bedroom flats on three storeys.** |
| Timescale for completion of construction: | **Six months from possession of the site.** |

### 3. The existing environment

**The site is a green field site originally owned by British Rail. It is bordered to the south by a main railway line to London and to the east by a busy local distributor road.**

**The site used to sustain a small electricity substation of which only the concrete slab and gravel areas remain.**

**The area is very busy. Due to the bend and bridge piers, delivery of material will be difficult and construction traffic will cause a hazard to road users.**

**If cranes are used, there will be no slewing above the railway without written permission from Railtrack.**

**There is a deep sewer (five metres below ground level) which will require careful consideration.**

### 4. Existing drawings

*Not applicable.*

### 5. The design

**The main hazard identified in the construction of the project for which provision has to be made is the deep excavation for the connection of the drainage system into the public sewer.**

---

* In this example plan, the case study designer's inputs to the plan are shown in bold face, while the inputs of others are shown in italics.

The contractor is required to submit proposals for management during construction of the following:

- temporary protection measures for working adjacent to railway

- procedures for off-loading materials and the placing of concrete beams

- submission of cranes to be used to obtain Railtrack approval

- deep excavation in connection with drainage system.

## 6.       Construction materials

The scabbling of concrete and the necessity of cutting chases in brick or blockwork walls has been removed.  However, should any such activity be necessary during construction, the principal contractor is to provide all necessary protection from dust.

## 7.       Site wide elements

- the main hazard identified is the site access and egress.  The precise position of the cross-over is identified on the drawings.

- location of welfare facilities during construction.

## 8.       Overlap with client's undertaking

*Not applicable.*

## 9.       Site Rules

Site to be kept clean and dust to be controlled.  No loud playing of radios which may cause disturbance to neighbours.

## 10.      Continuing liaison

*Procedures for consideration and acceptance of the health and safety implications of design elements of the principal contractor's and other contractors' packages are as follows:*

- *submit details of the health and safety issues to the planning supervisor, together with the results of risk assessment.*

*Procedures for dealing with unforeseen eventualities during project execution resulting in substantial design changes and which might affect resources:*

- *as soon as an unforeseen eventuality arises, the planning supervisor is to be informed*
- *health and safety issues arising are to be submitted as soon as reasonably practicable after the occurrence*
- *details of redesign and the health and safety implications are to be submitted for consideration in good time before execution.*

## 5.8   THE HEALTH AND SAFETY FILE

The file should contain:

1. Site survey

2. Copies of all general arrangement drawings produced by the architect

3. Copies of all drawings produced by the structural engineer showing all structural elements

4. Drawings showing general dispositions of concrete beams and pots

5. Materials used in external and internal walling

6. Position of all electrical control equipment and water stop cocks, and location of all services on site and in building

7. Drainage layout and manhole schedule

8. Maintenance manuals.

# 6 Tower block overcladding during occupation

## 6.1 INTRODUCTION

This example is based on an actual tower block external envelope refurbishment project and illustrates a two-stage design development leading to the preparation of tender documents at the end of the detailed design stage.

For a project of this type a concept design is followed immediately by detailed design. At that point the planning supervisor will have ensured the preparation of the pre-tender stage health and safety plan from the information provided by the design team whom he had a duty to co-ordinate in relation to health and safety matters.

This case study deals with the two design stages in turn, briefly addressing the health and safety issues and the associated hazards. The CDM principle of communicating a health and safety plan from design to construction has been reflected back into the design process and adopted between each design stage. The concept design stage identifies the health and safety issues that need to be carried forward and addressed at the detailed design stage.

## 6.2 PROJECT INFORMATION

### 6.2.1 Description and location

The project involves an 11 storey block of local authority flats built circa 1960.

The block is constructed of pebbledash, rendered in-situ, concrete walls on a reinforced concrete frame, with precast reinforced concrete cladding panels to certain elevations.

Windows are steel casement and some flats have small projecting concrete balconies.

The 44 flats are served by a single staircase and two passenger lifts.

The roof is flat with tank and lift motor rooms etc.

The block is located on a fairly open grassed site between two minor roads.

Vehicular access to the block is from one of the minor roads. This is used for refuse collection and access to parking areas etc. The other blocks have similar and separate access arrangements.

### 6.2.2 Client requirements

The block suffers from the following problems:

- unattractive and 'municipal' appearance
- poor thermal performance due to single glazed windows and mass concrete walls
- cold bridging due to projecting concrete balconies, leading to isolated condensation.

In addition there is an accumulation of items of disrepair:

- defective roof coverings to main roof and plant/tank rooms
- spalling concrete to reinforced concrete elements
- defective pebbledash render leading to falling debris and water penetration
- defective jointing to p.c. and r.c. cladding panels
- corrosion and distortion to steel casement windows generally and to glazed screens to main staircase and sidelights to cross ventilated lobbies at each landing
- deterioration of finishes etc. to internal common parts.

The brief was, therefore, to address each of the above issues in the most cost-effective way, having regard to the fact that the tenants would remain in occupation throughout the project.

Selected solutions should also address the question of future maintenance.

No existing drawings or reports on the construction of the block are available. Therefore, investigations will be necessary to establish its exact construction in order to design adequate fixings to support the weight of any externally applied cladding, either by a rainscreen system or rendered elevations.

### 6.2.3    The design team

The lead designer on this particular project is a chartered building surveyor. At concept design stage advice will be sought from a structural engineer with regard to the construction of the block and its ability to withstand the additional loads associated with any form of cladding, suitable fixings, etc.

The scheme will then be developed by the lead consultant who will ultimately prepare tender documents. These will specify the overcladding system by performance, in accordance with EC requirements. The detailed design of the overcladding system will then be prepared by the specialist cladding system manufacturer's own engineers, whose input with regard to health and safety issues will be co-ordinated by the planning supervisor.

## 6.3   CONCEPT DESIGN STAGE

### 6.3.1   Discussion of health and safety issues

The following health and safety matters must be considered:

1.    The block stands on an open grassed site thus requiring specific measures to prevent access by the general public to work activity and materials.

2.    The relatively exposed nature of the site will require special consideration with regard to the wind effect on protective screens, handling of materials, etc.

3.    The block has one principal point of ingress and egress with two secondary exits on the flanks. In addition, half of the flats have private balconies accessed by doors from the living rooms, thus penetrating the zone of activity to be occupied by any contractor working on the external envelope.

4.    The block has a low perimeter parapet to the roof which is only accessible for maintenance. Edge protection during the works must be provided.

5.    The present configuration of the opening portions of windows makes them difficult to clean

without 'overreaching' from inside. Some windows, particularly to the common parts, can only be cleaned using external access arrangements.

6. The performance of the windows needs to comply with the appropriate British Standards, having regard to the wind and rain exposure level.

7. Build-up of previous paint finishes to the common staircase and approach lobbies represents an existing hazard, recognised since the Kings Cross fire, as rapid surface spread of flame can occur. Removal of paint by whatever means will have COSHH implications. Liaison with the Fire Officer will be required.

8. There is no overhead or underground service which is likely to present a hazard when erecting scaffolding or carrying out any future works.

9. Because of the size and configuration of the block, consideration must be given to 'works' access and how operatives and heavy/awkward materials are taken to the workplace.

10. Repairs and improvements to the external elevations of the block will involve extensive scaffolding and relatively noisy operations with associated vibrations, dust, etc. Similarly, the removal of existing paint finishes from the common staircase and approach lobbies can only be carried out by chemical or mechanical means, both involving potential health hazards to the occupants of the building. In the event of a fire breaking out in any one of the flats, the staircase would need to be available for safe escape at any time during the contract.

It is clear, therefore, that such work would ideally be carried out in a vacant building in order to minimise risk to the Council's tenants. However, the Local Authority concerned does not have the decant resource to achieve even partial vacation. Therefore, the health and safety plan must address the safety of the occupants of the building as well as of the contractor's workforce etc.

The various design concepts are then reviewed.

## Roof

Option 1:    Strip and recover in asphalt on tapered insulation to improve thermal performance and falls.

*H & S issues:*

- ensure adequate edge protection during installation
- locate asphalt plant to reduce transportation of hot/molten asphalt
- locate gas bottles in association with asphalt plant. Ensure secure storage of gas bottles
- address fire risk inherent in 'hot works'
- COSHH issues with regard to insulation board
- consider physical dimensions of boards with regard to handling in high winds.

*H & S assessment:*

- this is work routinely carried out and the hazards are familiar to competent designers and contractors.

Option 2:    Construction of pitched roof with lightweight 'tile profile' covering on timber trusses.

*H & S issues:*

- installation of pitched roof on 11 storey block
- future maintenance of roof and rainwater system
- need for temporary roof to protect occupants from water ingress during construction.

*H & S assessment:*

• work not routinely carried out at such a height, although design issues familiar to competent designers and contractors.

*Recommendations:*

The retention of the flat roof is recommended on economic and health and safety grounds and the health and safety issues identified above are to be incorporated in the concept design stage of the health and safety plan.

### External envelope

Option 1:    Improve thermal performance by installation of dry lining internally. Address external appearance by concrete repair procedures and external decoration of previously undecorated surfaces.

*H & S issues:*

• increased interface with occupants of building
• access for concrete repairs and decoration
• concrete removal and grit blasting associated with comprehensive concrete repair project
• regular access to elevations required for cyclical redecoration
• protection of building occupants - safe ingress/egress.

*H & S assessment:*

• work routinely carried out and hazards are familiar to competent designers and contractors.

Option 2:    External insulation to walls with render system to provide weather resistance and decorative surface. Introduction of insulation to exposed surface of balconies etc.

*H & S issues:*

• access for reduced concrete repairs but required for application of insulation and render
• COSHH issues with regard to insulation and render mortars
• drilling of elevations to fix insulation and mesh for rendering (noise/vibration/dust)
• future maintenance of render
• hazard of falling render in the event of future failure
• asphalting to private balconies - see H & S consideration for main roof asphalting
• protection of building occupants - safe ingress/egress.

*H & S assessment:*

• work routinely carried out and hazards are familiar to competent designers and contractors.

Option 3:    Installation of 'rainscreen' cladding system to third to 11th floors inclusive, with render system to lower two floors. Introduction of insulation to exposed surfaces of balconies to avoid cold bridging.

*H & S issues:*

• access with clearance to allow for installation of support system and cladding panels
• fixing of insulation behind rainscreen system and related COSHH issues

- future maintenance and cleaning of rainscreen system
- hazard of falling rainscreen panels in event of fixing failure
- limited concrete repairs and work to rendering prior to fixing of rainscreen system
- drilling of concrete elements for rainscreen system support fixings (noise/vibration/dust)
- ensure integrity of lightning protection during installation and afterwards
- asphalting to private balconies - see H & S consideration for main roof asphalting
- protection of building occupants - safe ingress/egress.

*H & S assessment:*

- work routinely carried out and hazards are familiar to competent 'specialist' designers and contractors.

*Recommendations:*

Installation of a rainscreen system is recommended on economic and aesthetic grounds. None of the health and safety issues identified is sufficient to exclude any of the options.

The special hazards associated with the rainscreen installation have been identified and will be incorporated in the concept design stage health and safety plan.

### Windows

Option 1:              Overhaul existing windows and install secondary double glazing.

*H & S issues:*

- access
- interface with occupants
- de-glazing (windows cannot be de-glazed without breaking panes) and grit blasting in order to overhaul existing frames etc. Protection of tenants/chattels
- COSHH implications with regard to new paint system
- future maintenance of paint system on 11 storey building
- configuration of opening portions of windows still unsuitable for internal cleaning
- reglazing.

*H & S assessment*

- work routinely carried out and hazards are familiar to competent designers and contractors, although special care needs to be taken with in-situ grit blasting.

Option 2:              Renew windows with double glazed units of either uPVC or aluminium. Revise configuration of opening portions to allow internal cleaning.

*H & S issues:*

- access
- interface with occupants
- removal of old windows:
    - from opening
    - from scaffold
- future maintenance of long-life units
- reglazing.

*H & S assessment:*

- work routinely carried out and hazards are familiar to competent designers and contractors.

*Recommendations:*

It is recommended that on economic and aesthetic grounds the windows are replaced with double glazed, powder coated, aluminium casement windows of revised configuration. There are no overriding health and safety issues during construction; however, installing new windows raises fewer health and safety issues during cleaning and maintenance. Modern locking and opening limiters will improve safety for children as well as security against intruders.

### Redecoration of common parts

In view of the build-up of previous paint finishes, no further decoration can be undertaken in view of the existing and inherent hazards. Therefore, all existing finishes must be removed back to the substrate.

*H & S issues:*

- interface with occupants
- COSHH aspects of removal system to be adopted
- ventilation requirements during removal process
- control of access and maintenance of means of escape/programme of work in the single staircase building.

*H & S assessment:*

- work routinely carried out by specialist sub-contractor, but not routinely carried out under direction of most principal contractors.

Contractors will be asked to propose a method statement for removing the existing finishes, taking due note of the ventilation requirements and the possibility that the staircase will be a 'confined space'.

It is of particular importance that the method statement explains how the staircase is to be kept available for means of escape at all times during the contract and the paint stripping process. As the major fire risk occurs at night, the staircase must be returned to a satisfactory state of cleanliness and illumination and be totally unobstructed. During the day the staircase must be maintained in use and any obstruction must be kept to a minimum. Operatives must be in attendance at all times.

The recommended options for the work sections identified will be carried forward to the detailed design stage when the health and safety issues will be addressed in more detail.

## 6.3.2 Designer's contribution to the health and safety plan and file

### The design issues

The design issues related to the various options available have been considered at the concept design stage and the following options selected:

- renewal of asphalt flat roof coverings with tapered insulation to achieve falls
- installation of insulated and ventilated rainscreen system incorporating cavity barriers etc. to upper nine storeys, with render system to lower two storeys
- replacement of existing steel casement windows with powder coated aluminium casements (double glazed)
- redecoration of common parts internally etc. following removal of existing finishes back to substrate.

'F' in the right-hand margin denotes an item which should be incorpoarated in the project file and 'P' an item to be included in the plan.

### Recommendations

It is recommended that in the preparation of the detailed design, consideration is given to the following issues.

The safety and convenience of the occupants must be the prime concern for all operatives. This will affect common access/egress areas and individual flats.

1.  The roof perimeter parapet is increased in height to provide future edge protection                   P/F
2.  In view of the future weather protection to be afforded to the block by the rainscreen system, non-intrusive concrete repair systems are investigated                   -
3.  Design of rainscreen system, to utilise handleable cladding panels of reasonable size with easily identifiable and removable fixings for future maintenance                   P/F
4.  Consider installation of roof-mounted cradle track for future elevational access for cleaning etc.                   F
5.  Alternatively, consider provision of 'tying-in' points for future scaffold or access towers                   P/F
6.  Review new window designs to ensure cleanability and investigate practicality of internal glazing                   P/F
7.  Give consideration to alternative method of paint removal within common parts, e.g. abrasive removal, cf. chemical stripping and relative ventilation requirements of both. If chemical stripping selected, specify COSHH friendly system (Note: Details of the exact finish applied and of how it can be maintained and subsequently removed needs to be included within the file)                   P/F
8.  Obtain hazard data sheets for all specified materials, e.g. insulation board, adhesives, etc.                   P/F

## 6.4   DETAILED DESIGN STAGE

### 6.4.1   Health and safety issues

At the concept design stage the various design options were considered and decisions taken. Hence the main objective for health and safety at the detailed design stage is to reduce the effects of known hazards and achieve control during the construction work.

**Review design concepts and key issues**

The health and safety issues identified in relation to each of the major work sections are reiterated below:

### Roof

*   ensure adequate edge protection during installation                   P
*   locate asphalt plant to reduce transportation of hot/molten asphalt                   P
*   locate gas bottles in association with asphalt plant and ensure secure storage of gas bottles                   P
*   address fire risk inherent in 'hot works'                   P
*   COSHH issues with regard to insulation board                   P/F
*   consider handling characteristics of insulation board in the event of high winds.                   P

### External Envelope

- access with clearance to allow for installation of support system and cladding panels — P
- method of removing scaffolding as elevations covered in cladding material — P/F
- identification of removable cladding panels for future scaffold fixing — P/F
- method of transporting materials to the workface — P
- prevention of unauthorised access to scaffold — P
- protective fans over block entrances to protect the public and tenants — P
- fixing of insulation behind rainscreen system and related COSHH issues — P/F
- future maintenance and cleaning of rainscreen system — F
- hazard of falling rainscreen panels in event of fixing failure — F
- limited concrete repairs and work to rendering prior to fixing of rainscreen system — -
- drilling of concrete elements for rainscreen system support fixings (dust etc.) — P
- ensure integrity of lightning protection during installation and after — P
- asphalting to private balconies - see H & S consideration for main roof asphalting. — P

### Windows

- access — P
- interface with occupants — P
- removal of old windows:
    - from structural opening — P
    - from scaffold to ground level for disposal — P
- method of transporting new windows to the workface — P
- future maintenance of new units — F
- type of glass, e.g. shatter-proof etc. — P/F
- reglazing in the event of future breakage. — F

### Redecoration of common parts

- interface with occupants — P
- COSHH aspects with regard to removal system to be adopted — P
- ventilation requirements during removal process — P
- control of access and maintenance of means of escape/programme of work in the single staircase building. — P/F

From examination of the hazards identified, various specific issues can be addressed at design stage, e.g. configuration of opening portions of windows for future cleaning and maintenance, future repair of glazing from inside flats.

The maintenance of the staircase by day and night as a means of access/egress for the occupants is crucial to the safety of the scheme. It is also apparent that the access arrangements must be capable of serving a wide variety of construction needs, i.e. concrete repairs, renewal of windows, installation of rainscreen system and roof access for transportation of roof re-covering/insulation materials.

There are conflicting requirements for the temporary access system needed for the removal of the windows (scaffold boarded to the face of the building) and for the installation of the rainscreen cladding system (working zone between face of building and scaffold).

All these matters will be addressed in the health and safety plan to be prepared by the tendering contractors.

**Identify maintenance and repair strategy for each work section:**

- frequency of maintenance inspections
- maintenance access

- materials of maintenance and repairs
- input into the health and safety file.

**Identify demolition hazards:**

- input into the health and safety file.

## 6.5  THE BUILDING SURVEYOR'S CONTRIBUTION TO THE PRE-TENDER STAGE HEALTH AND SAFETY PLAN*

### 1.  General

All prospective main contractors tendering for this contract will receive this skeletal health and safety plan.  The purpose is to highlight the main health and safety issues in connection with the construction work on the project and to form the basis for tenderers to explain their proposals for managing the problems.

### 2.  Nature of project

Name of client:  **A Local Authority**

Location:  **Uncongested suburban residential site**

The construction work:  **The construction work entails the renewal of roof coverings incorporating insulation, the renewal of windows, the carrying out of various concrete repairs, installation of a rainscreen overcladding system to the upper storeys.**

**Works also include the redecoration and prior removal of existing paint finishes to the common staircase and dwelling approach lobbies.**

**Throughout the project the building will be occupied by local authority tenants and this will prove a major constraint on operations.**

Timescale for completion
of construction work:  **The proposed timescale for the work is eight months.**

### 3.  The existing environment

**The block is located on a fairly open grassed site between two minor roads.**

**Vehicular access to the block is from one of the minor roads and is used for refuse collection and access to parking areas etc.  This must be maintained since the tenants will remain in occupation.**

---

* In this example plan, the case study designer's inputs to the plan are shown in bold face, while the inputs of others are shown in italics.

## 4.    Existing drawings

**Drawings prepared as a result of surveys are listed in Appendix A.**  (Not included here)

## 5.    The design

The following principal hazards or works sequences so far identified cannot be avoided and will be a risk to health and safety of construction workers and/or the occupants of, or visitors to, the building.  These can be divided into two categories:

(a) where standard solutions apply and will minimise and control risks.
(b) where standard solutions do not apply and special provisions are required.

Note that standard solutions are not hazard free.

The specific hazards and assessed risks are outlined below for each work section affected and designated as (a) or (b).  The list does not address the commonplace hazards which must be controlled by site management good practice.

It will be the responsibility of a competent contractor to detail their proposals for managing these problems.  These details/method statements will be incorporated into the health and safety plan prior to the work commencing on site.

### Roof - General Items

* *temporary work for renewing roof coverings regarding inadequate existing edge protection on occupied block* (a)
* *'hot working' with asphalt - gas bottles etc.* (a)

### Envelope

* *access and working space required for installation of rainscreen* (b)
* *protection of occupants and operatives during concrete repair works* (a)
* *protection of operatives and occupants during re-asphalting of private balconies* (a)
* *drilling concrete for rainscreen support fixing.* (a)

### Windows

* *protection of operatives and occupants during removal of existing windows from building and removal from site* (a)
* *access arrangements for window renewal having regard to constraints placed upon access arrangements for insulation of rainscreen system.* (b)

### Redecoration of common parts

* *removal of existing paint finishes by abrasive or chemical means within staircase of single staircase building occupied during contract.* (b)

In all of the above instances the contractor is required to submit detailed proposals and method statements as part of the tender submission.

## 6.    Construction materials

The following health hazards from materials have been identified which cannot be avoided and which will be a risk to the health of workers and occupants during construction:

- **insulation boards installed behind rainscreen system and rendering of lower storeys**
- **specialist epoxy mortars used in rendering system to lower storeys and balcony elevation walls**
- **anti-graffiti coatings to common parts and staircase enclosure.**

## 7.    Site wide elements

The following hazards have been identified which will be a risk to the safety of occupants of the building:

- **ingress and egress from the residential block and separation of occupants from building operations.**

The following hazards have been identified which will be a risk to the safety of construction workers:

- **site access and egress having regard to proximity of small roundabout.**

It will be the responsibility of the contractor to detail their proposals for managing these problems. These details/method statements will be incorporated into the health and safety plan prior to the work commencing on site.

## 8.    Overlap with client's undertaking

**It must be acknowledged and accepted by the principal contractor that the block is to remain occupied by council tenants throughout the duration of the contract and that all existing services, television reception arrangements, etc. must be maintained.**

*Specific provision must be made for the protection of tenants and their children whilst entering and leaving the block and whilst using the staircase, particularly for means of escape when paint stripping in progress.*

It will be the responsibility of the contractor to detail their proposals for managing these problems. These details/method statements will be incorporated into the health and safety plan prior to the work commencing on site.

## 9.    Site Rules

The following rules have been devised to control the risks arising from the identified hazards:

- **site permits to be obtained by all persons entering that part of the site controlled by the contractor, e.g. site compound, storage areas, scaffold.**
- **separation of tenants/tenants' children from workface etc.**

## 10.    Continuing liaison

Procedures for consideration and acceptance of the health and safety implications of design elements of the principal contractor and other contractors' packages are as follows:

- *submit details of the health and safety issues to the planning supervisor, including results of appropriate risk assessments*
- *implications arising from the design of access arrangements in particular will be required well in advance of the execution of the work to allow full consideration.*

Procedures for dealing with unforeseen eventualities during project execution which result in substantial design changes and which might affect resources are as follows:

- *as soon as an unforeseen eventuality arises, the planning supervisor is to be informed*
- *the health and safety issues arising from the eventuality are to be notified by the contractor as soon as possible after the occurrence with proposals for dealing with them*
- *details of the redesign and the health and safety implications are to be submitted for consideration and acceptance in due time before execution.*

Account should be taken in the works programme of:

- *overlapping and conflicting operations*
- *work that directly affects occupants*
- *liaison with Fire Officer regarding escape staircase.*

## 6.6    THE HEALTH AND SAFETY FILE

The necessary details with regard to future maintenance or demolition to be included in the health and safety file are set out below:

### *Roof*

Future maintenance must recognise the following:

- the presence of foamglass insulation beneath the asphalt
- the presence of a half brick perimeter wall against which the asphalt upstand is formed
- that to gain access to the upstand wall and to properly detail future re-asphalting it will be necessary to drill out the fixing rivets and remove the apron weathering. During such an operation rain would be able to penetrate behind the rainscreen system but will not penetrate the building and therefore no special precautions with regard to weather tightness need be made.

### *External Envelope*

*Installation details*

The rainscreen system is supplied by (name company) and the design and installation drawings and schedules are as follows:

List details

*Maintenance of services*

External gas risers are concealed behind the rainscreen system in a location shown on the drawings. To access these, the cladding panels can be removed by taking off the plastic cover caps and drilling out the fixing rivets. The panels can be refitted by reversing this process.

Overflows from individual WWPs etc. within the flats are also taken down behind the rainscreen system to emerge at a manifold at second floor slab level. The cladding panels can be removed as above for future access.

In any future maintenance or demolition of the rainscreen system, the presence of glass fibre insulation must be recognised. The void behind the rainscreen cladding is ventilated at top and bottom, with perforated steel fire stops with intumescent linings at each storey level.
In the event of fire damage it will be necessary to replace any damaged boards, aluminium support system and intumescent fire stops.

Product data sheets are enclosed for:

- the glass fibre insulation
- the render system at ground and first floor levels.

### Windows and common parts

Product data sheets are enclosed for:

- the windows, detailing methods of re-glazing, cleaning etc.
- the product used for redecorating the staircase, listing cleaning and maintenance processes.

In the event of future stripping of the finishes within the common parts to prevent further film build-up, reference should be made to the original contractor's method statement setting up the following:

- adequacy of ventilation
- COSHH Statement with regard to products used
- maintenance of means of escape etc. during work.

# 7 Refurbishment of building engineering services

## 7.1 INTRODUCTION

This example has been prepared from an engineering services consultant's viewpoint. It is intended to illustrate the building services engineer's considerations of health and safety issues during the various stages of a project from conception through to final design, and to highlight their input into the health and safety plan and file. This example has been produced as the hypothetical extension of a real project which had reached feasibility stage.

The design is progressed through three stages:

* concept
* outline
* detailed.

In a project of this nature, there will need to be significant interaction between the services engineer(s), other members of the design team and the planning supervisor throughout the design process.

The decision process as documented in this example involves considerable professional judgement and is inherently a form of risk assessment. No formal tabulated risk assessment has been included in this instance. The discussion of the decisions as presented could equally be documented in a tabulated risk assessment format, if this is considered more appropriate in the circumstances of any particular project.

## 7.2 PROJECT INFORMATION

### 7.2.1 Site description

A private client has acquired existing buildings which formed part of an old hospital site with a view to converting these into an elderly persons' residential home. The remaining areas of the site have been sold separately to a housing developer.

Three buildings form the client's acquisition:

* a central three storey block, formerly used as ground floor offices, staff facilities and entrance area, first and second floor ward areas - divided into two, three and four bedded rooms - with a partial basement used as a plant room housing a HWS storage calorifier and other equipment
* an adjacent, linked two storey block, formerly used as open ward areas
* an adjacent, linked single storey block, formerly used for staff areas, back-up services and storage.

The existing configuration is indicated on the key plan and section shown in Figures 7 and 8.

The single and three storey blocks are of late Victorian origin whilst the two storey block is a 1950s extension incorporating stairs and a bed lift.

The buildings have not been in use or maintained for the last two years.

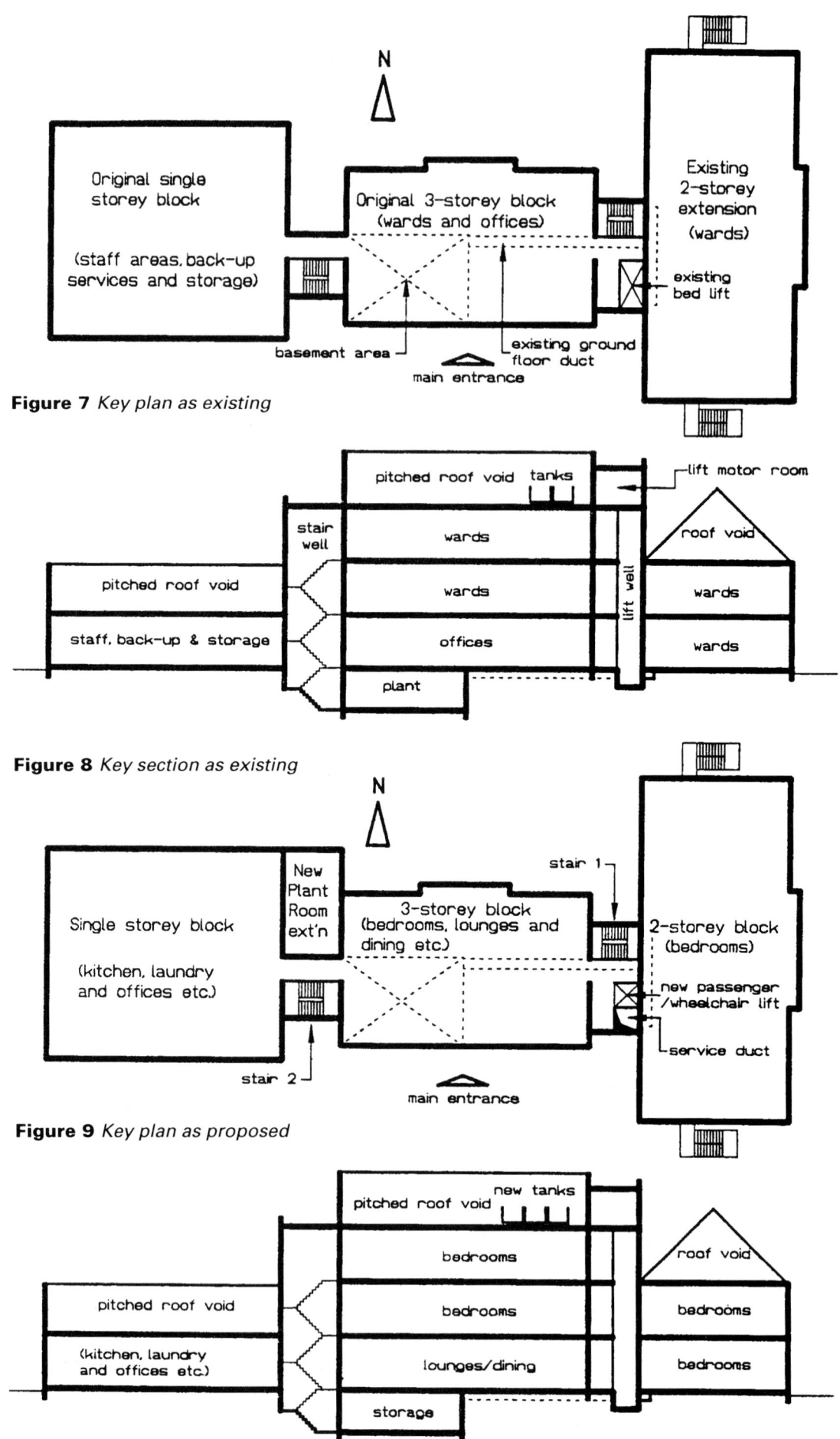

**Figure 7** *Key plan as existing*

**Figure 8** *Key section as existing*

**Figure 9** *Key plan as proposed*

**Figure 10** *Key section as proposed*

They were serviced from the remote main hospital boiler house and substation which have been decommissioned, together with the basement calorifier plant.

### 7.2.2 Client requirements

The client wishes to retain the existing buildings and convert these as economically as possible into residential accommodation for the elderly, comprising a minimum of 42 bedroom units with en-suite bathroom facilities, communal sitting and dining rooms, kitchen, laundry, offices and staff facilities.

These requirements are indicated on the key plan and section shown in Figures 9 and 10.

The estimated cost of the project is £1.7m.

### 7.2.3 Local environment

The site is reasonably level with good access from an adjacent main road. The area surrounding the site is being developed as housing. There is no inherent problem associated with the site location or conditions from the viewpoint of the services engineer.

## 7.3 CONCEPT DESIGN STAGE

### 7.3.1 Scope of engineering services work/programme

'F' in the right-hand margin denotes an item which should be incorporated in the project file and 'P' an item to be included in the plan.

The works within the engineering services consultant's brief, referenced to the National Engineering Specification groupings, comprise:

- (R) Disposal systems - above ground drainage
- (S) Piped supply systems - hot and cold water services, gas, hydrant and hose reel systems
- (T) Mechanical heating/cooling/refrigeration systems - boilers and heating system
- (U) Ventilation/air conditioning systems - bathroom/toilet extract ventilation and kitchen ventilation
- (V) Electrical supply/power/lighting - internal power and lighting systems and external lighting
- (W) Communication/security/control systems - fire detection and alarm systems, telephone, tv and cctv services, and call system
- (X) Transport systems - lift installation.                                    P

A programme for the provision of information for the health and safety plan has been agreed with the planning supervisor.

### 7.3.2 Discussion of health and safety issues and hazards related to the engineering services works

*Review of design issues taking into account health and safety aspects, hazards, risk assessment and the application of the principles of prevention and protection*

Initial studies have shown that other development possibilities, such as finding a suitable green field site for a purpose-built building, are economically unacceptable to the client.

The alternatives of refurbishment, or demolition and rebuilding have been compared. Both possibilities involve the hazards associated with stripping out and disposal of services and plant. Total demolition would introduce general demolition hazards, e.g. risk of falls, collapse of materials, dust, noise, etc.

Refurbishment introduces hazards associated with:

- additional surveys/inspections
- the location of new plant and equipment in relation to the restrictions imposed by the existing building layout and construction
- the adaptation of existing services and plant where appropriate, i.e. cutting, burning, welding, etc.

Having considered the balance of health and safety risks in these two alternatives, together with meeting the client's objectives, aesthetics and buildability, against the relative costs resulting from health and safety incidents (including potential accidents, delays, etc.), it has been decided to proceed on the basis of refurbishment. It is recognised that significant hazards remain which will need to be assessed carefully by the designer during the development of the design to try to avoid or, where this is not possible, to reduce the risks to the health and safety of all those involved in further investigation, construction, maintenance, repair and eventual dismantling or demolition.

The age of the building suggests a likelihood of the presence of asbestos which would pose a health hazard both during survey and construction stages of the project. An initial specialist inspection and sampling exercise should, therefore, be arranged and its findings/ recommendations made known prior to the commencement of detailed survey work within the building. P

The design team have studied the records of the previous owner, the gas, electricity, water, National Rivers and local authorities and the asbestos register. P/F

### *Primary health and safety hazards inherent to the site, neighbourhood and nature of the engineering services work:*

- condition of existing buildings/site P
- location and access to existing services and plant P
- removal and disposal of existing services and plant. P

### *Principal hazards:*

- hazardous substances and materials relating to previous use and the condition of existing buildings, i.e. infectious diseases, needles, gases, asbestos, lead, radioactive waste, dust and dirt, substances in ventilation ductwork (particularly extract), vermin, etc. Consideration should also be given to environmental hazards from existing substances and materials, e.g. refrigerants P

- safety hazards relating to condition of existing buildings and access to existing plant and services, i.e. electrical safety, live gas services (including medical gases), pressurised pipelines, legionella in stored water, confined spaces, falls, etc. P

- health and safety hazards associated with the installation, future maintenance and repair of services, plant and equipment, i.e. confined spaces, falls, musculo-skeletal injuries from manual handling, etc. P

### *Initial assessment of the health and safety knowledge*

The engineering services designer is familiar with the nature of the existing building services and the proposed installation work. It is assumed that the services engineering designer has proved his competence and resources to the satisfaction of the client and his planning supervisor.

Requirements for the contractor's familiarity with this type of work, in particular the stripping out of any existing services and plant, must also be considered.

### Action required

Health and safety issues are to be recorded in the health and safety plan to ensure consideration at subsequent stages of the design and construction process. Any information for inclusion in the health and safety file should be logged and stored where necessary.

Safe working procedures must be established for surveyors, etc. entering the premises to locate and identify existing services. Check that Health Authority clearance certificate is available or arrange for specialist clearance and certification of premises.

## 7.3.3    Designer's contributions to health and safety plan

### The existing environment

#### Existing services

No overhead services but underground services require investigation.

#### Existing buildings

Careful consideration must be given to the health and safety of surveyors/inspectors entering the existing buildings or inspecting services, i.e. drainage. They must be made aware of, and protected from, any potentially harmful substances and materials. Tests for gases (e.g. $CO_2$, methane, etc.) should be carried out in all confined spaces and ducts prior to entry. Check that the health clearance certificate for the premises has been issued by Health Authority. Detailed investigation to be undertaken to identify and record the location and extent of hazardous substances and materials prior to further survey work.

#### Ground conditions

Check that investigation is planned since underground service alterations are likely to be required which would expose workers to potential risk from collapse of excavations, contamination or contact with live services.

### Existing drawings

Investigate availability of existing record drawings and information, in particular in relation to services both in the buildings and externally above and below ground. Expect data to be incomplete and inaccurate and plan accordingly for thorough surveys.

### The design

Hazards and work sequences which are likely to pose a risk to the health and safety of construction workers are as detailed in Section 7.3.2 - Principal hazards.

Specific activities where contractors will have to explain their proposals for managing the work will be:

- stripping out, dismantling and disposal of existing services, plant and equipment
- installation of major items of plant and equipment
- fire precautions for hot working methods
- testing, flushing and chemical cleaning/treatment of services
- commissioning.

## 7.4   OUTLINE DESIGN STAGE

### 7.4.1   Scope of engineering services work

The works within the engineering services consultant's brief remain as before (see Section 7.3.1) but will require amplification/clarification during the development of the design, in particular distinguishing between services to be retained, altered or extended, and new services.

### 7.4.2   Issues and hazards relating to engineering services works

*Review of major health and safety issues, hazards, risk assessment and the application of the principles of prevention and protection relating to construction/ installation and commissioning techniques necessitated by the engineering services design*

*Access/egress*

The size of the main central plant and boilers, together with the installation access requirements, indicate that the existing basement calorifier room, which has limited headroom, is likely to be inadequate.  The alternatives are:

* lowering the basement floor to provide adequate headroom
* allocating an alternative area at another floor level within the building
* constructing a new boiler house/plant room.

A detailed risk assessment has been carried out and a précis follows.

The lowering of the existing basement floor would require extensive structural alterations, including underpinning of foundations, etc. which would introduce significant additional health and safety hazards during construction.  Space within the building is at a premium in order to meet the client's accommodation requirements.  On balance, the construction of a new boiler house/ plant room would offer significant advantages in providing purpose-designed accommodation with ease of access.

Investigations have shown that the existing water storage cisterns in the roof space of the three storey block are severely corroded and beyond repair. The cisterns currently contain water at ambient temperature and must therefore be checked for legionella. Additional cistern capacity may be necessary to meet the requirements of the new use of the buildings, although this should be minimised to reduce the likelihood of legionella.  Improved permanent access to the cistern area is considered essential as this will not only allow easier removal of existing cisterns and installation of new ones, but also facilitate regular maintenance.

An alternative of using a pressurised/unvented system with cisterns and pumps at ground floor level was considered.  It has been decided that this system should not be pursued on the grounds of increased installation and running costs and the potential risk of pressure/blending problems in operation.                                                                                                     P

*Demolition (stripping out)*

A specialist investigation has identified asbestos insulation in the basement calorifier room.  No further asbestos was found.  A contract will therefore have to be set up with a specialist licensed asbestos removal contractor and the HSE must be informed.  Consideration must be given to the impact of this work on the overall programming of the works.                                                          P

Large amounts of existing pipework will need to be removed. Most of this is painted and some may be galvanised which will require special precautions during removal. Burning techniques should be avoided where reasonably possible, since these are likely to create toxic fumes and the risk of fire. The age of the building indicates a likelihood of lead pipework. Precautions must, therefore, be taken for handling lead. Record drawings cannot be located for all existing piped services. All pipework will need to be purged prior to removal to ensure that it is cleared of hazardous gases and substances.                                                                                                P

The clearing of the existing galvanised steel cisterns from the roof space will present health and safety hazards for the contractor as they will have to be cut up for removal through the existing roof access openings. Alternative openings to allow removal in one piece should be considered, since burning methods will present health hazards due to the toxic gases produced, and mechanical cutting will be both time-consuming and present fire and musculo-skeletal hazards. Consultation will be necessary with other members of the design team and planning supervisor.  P

Removal of the existing extract ductwork will require analysis of internal deposits before the work is undertaken and disposal arranged.                                                                                                P

The removal and disposal of existing lighting fittings will need to take account of the carcinogenic properties of pcbs and the requirements for safe handling and disposal of fluorescent tubes.                                                                                                P

Care will be required to minimise the risks of fire, explosion and to health arising from the dust, dirt or other debris likely to be found in services ducts and floor, ceiling or roof voids.       P

### *Hazardous materials/substances*

Investigations have shown that the buildings have a health clearance certificate for infectious diseases, radioactive materials, etc. and that no piped medical gas supplies or pressurised pipelines exist.                                                                                                P/F

Dust, dirt and other debris in service ducts and floor, ceiling or roof voids could pose fire, explosion or health hazards during construction. Arrangements should be made for cleaning these areas.                                                                                                P

Storage cisterns, water pipework and hose reel systems must be purged/drained and chlorinated before re-use to reduce the risk of legionella. Cisterns should be provided with lids and insulated.                                                                                                P

Hazardous materials and substances necessitated by the design are to be identified (e.g. refrigerants).                                                                                                P

### *Fire*

The existing hose reel system will be retained in the refurbished building. This should be used   F to augment temporary fire fighting facilities during construction. The necessary arrangements must be made to ensure availability of water supply. Adequate signs must be provided regarding the use of hose reels.                                                                                                P

### *Review of major health and safety hazards relating to the maintenance, cleaning, repair, replacement, decommissioning, dismantling and disposal of the engineering plant, equipment and services installations*

### *Access requirements*

The decision to construct a new boiler house/plant room must be used as an opportunity to ensure

that adequate space is provided for the maintenance of plant and equipment without creating
risks to the health and safety of maintenance operatives.                                    F

The cistern installation in the roof space must be designed to ensure safe access, means of
emergency escape, safe access routes within the roof spaces, adequate lighting and ventilation.
Ease of access will facilitate regular monitoring and maintenance, thereby reducing the risks
from legionella.                                                                             F

The access provisions to and within the existing lift motor room have been checked in relation to
the alterations proposed to the lift and found to be adequate.

The locations of all service runs, light fittings, valves, control panels, fire dampers, smoke
detectors, etc. has been considered in relation to the ease and safety of access.

Major items of plant and equipment identified during the concept design stage have been
selected, taking into consideration their maintenance requirements in relation to the access
provisions.                                                                                  F

### Lifting requirements

The design will allow for plant and equipment to be sectionalised, where reasonably practicable,
to ease handling hazards during replacement.  The lifting of large or heavy items of plant and
equipment will be facilitated, where possible, by the provision of permanent lifting beams,
brackets or eyes built in to the structure.                                                  F

### Isolation requirements

Isolation provisions, including local arrangements, for plant, equipment and service runs in
relation to the potential maintenance, repair or replacement requirements will be incorporated into
the design to eliminate live working and its associated dangers.

### Re-assessment of the health and safety knowledge boundary

The engineering services designer's knowledge remains adequate.

Contractors familiar with stripping out potentially hazardous materials and with purging existing
services will be required.  Contractors must prove their competence and adequacy of their
resources.

### Action required

Health and safety issues are to be recorded in the health and safety plan to ensure consideration at
subsequent stages of the design and construction process. Any information for inclusion in the
health and safety file should be logged and stored where necessary.

Discuss any health and safety matters arising out of the issues considered to date with the planning
supervisor, highlighting those which affect other designers.

## 7.4.3    Designer's contribution to health and safety plan

Sections to be amplified as the health and safety plan develops are shown in square brackets [...].

### Nature of project

Nature of construction work:
[Define engineering services element of work].

Timescale for construction:
Allow for purging of services and removal of asbestos by specialist contractor.
[Consider co-ordination and rationalisation of different engineering trade contractors' activities].

### *The existing environment*

*Existing services:*

- there are no overhead services
- record drawings are available showing most underground services and some layout of internal services. These are incomplete and further detailed site investigation will be required to confirm the reliability of the existing information and the location and identity of other services
- all services have been isolated upon entry to the building, with the exception of [list]
- purging of existing pipework will be necessary prior to stripping out or alteration to eliminate the risks from any potentially hazardous substances
- painted, galvanised and lead pipework and cisterns exist which will require care to avoid creating toxic fumes and effects when these are removed, altered or extended.

*Existing traffic systems and restrictions:*

[Input required on plant and equipment sizes for delivery to site].

*Existing buildings:*

- a health clearance certificate for the buildings has been issued by Health Authority
- initial investigation has revealed asbestos insulation in basement, painted pipework and pcbs in light fittings and fluorescent lighting tubes. Detailed investigation to be undertaken to record the location and extent of these hazardous substances and materials
- dust, dirt and other debris should be expected in service ducts and floor, ceiling or roof voids. Appropriate control measures will be required during stripping out and cleaning must be carried out before the reinstatement of building engineering services
- protect surveyors/inspectors entering the existing buildings or inspecting services (i.e. drainage) from any potentially harmful substances and materials
- tests for gases (e.g. $CO_2$, methane, etc.) should be carried out in all confined spaces and ducts.

*Ground conditions:*

[A ground investigation is being planned to ensure that adequate information is available to prevent or reduce risks to workers from collapse of excavations, contamination or contact with live services during underground service alterations].

### *Existing drawings*

Available existing record drawings and information in relation to services in the buildings, externally above and below ground, and public utility services have been obtained. These do not document all known services, and additional site survey information is needed.

### *The design*

Hazards and work sequences which are likely to pose a risk to the health and safety of construction workers include:

- hazardous substances and materials relating to previous use and the condition of existing buildings, i.e. asbestos, painted, galvanised and lead pipework and water cisterns, pcbs and fluorescent tubes in light fittings, substances in extract ventilation ductwork, dust, dirt and other debris, etc.
- safety hazards relating to condition of existing buildings and access to existing plant and services, i.e. electrical safety, live gas services, legionella in stored water, confined spaces, falls, etc.

- health and safety hazards associated with the installation of services, plant and equipment, i.e. confined spaces, falls, musculo-skeletal injuries from manual handling, etc.

Provision has been made in the design for the existing hose reel system to remain live and be available for fire protection during construction.

Access improvements are included in the design to ease removal of existing cisterns in roof space.

[Further precautions and sequences of assembly, if any, needing to be followed during construction to be identified during the development of the design].

Specific activities for which contractors must detail their proposals for managing those aspects of the work are:

- asbestos removal
- purging of existing services
- stripping out, dismantling and disposal of existing services, plant and equipment
- installation of major items of plant and equipment
- fire precautions for hot working methods
- testing, flushing and chemical cleaning/treatment of services
- commissioning.

[Define requirements in more detail where appropriate].

### Construction materials

[Hazardous construction materials and substances must be identified during the development of the detailed design].

### Site wide elements

[Unloading and storage requirements for plant, equipment and other materials to be identified. Particular attention should be paid to the storage of any combustible materials or substances].

### Overlap with client's undertaking

The client will commence occupation of the premises one week prior to the completion of commissioning. All O & M manuals and 'as installed' drawings must be available in advance of this time.

### Site Rules

- restriction of access during asbestos removal, until clearance certificate issued
- conformity with all statutory requirements, including electricity at work, PPE at work, COSHH, noise at work, etc. regulations
- hot-working and confined space 'permit to work' systems required to comply with appropriate HSE and other recommendations
- control of contractors' activities during client occupation and commissioning.

### Continuing liaison

[Arrangements for contractor's design elements of work to identify, assess and document health and safety hazards and the appropriate preventative or protective measures to be set out during detailed design stage].

Contractors and suppliers will be required to provide equipment schedules, O & M manuals, 'as installed' information and identification measures.

## 7.5  DETAILED DESIGN STAGE

### 7.5.1  Scope of engineering services work

The works within the engineering services consultant's brief remain as before (see Section 7.3.1) but will require amplification/clarification during the development of the design, in particular distinguishing between services to be retained, altered or extended and new services, for inclusion in the health and safety plan.                                          P

### 7.5.2  Discussion of health and safety issues and hazards related to the engineering services works

*Review all health and safety issues, hazards, risk assessment and the application of the principles of prevention and protection relating to construction/installation and commissioning techniques necessitated by the engineering services design*

#### *Access/egress*

Design to be progressed adequately to enable all plant and equipment to be housed in new boiler house/plant room, switch rooms, motor room and tank rooms. All plant areas to be sized and arranged to allow adequate space, headroom and access for ease of installation and subsequent maintenance, etc. with lifting arrangements provided to avoid or minimise handling and musculo-skeletal hazards.

Sectionalise plant, equipment and cisterns, where reasonably practicable, to reduce installation handling hazards, e.g. new water cisterns to be installed in existing roof space and boilers to be sectional type suitable for in-situ assembly.                                          P/F

Bathroom/toilet ventilation system to be designed as individual units to ease installation problems and avoid need for large central extract units in roof space.

Adequate temporary lighting, power, and other supplies will be required in plant rooms, roof spaces, etc. to allow safe access for installation of plant, equipment and services.                                          P

#### *Demolition (stripping out)*

Prepare input into tender documentation for the asbestos removal contract, comprising drawings identifying the location of all known asbestos to be removed, together with details of any specific procedures to be followed for its safe removal and the legislation with which the contractor will have to comply. Advise planning supervisor on prequalification requirements of potential specialist contractors.                                          P

Prepare input into tender documentation for the general stripping out contract, comprising drawings identifying the location of all service runs, plant and equipment to be purged, details of services to be retained or removed, and details of the procedures required for safe removal and disposal of any hazardous materials or substances, including purge effluent. Consider any special provisions for access/egress requirements and for dealing with hazards from dust, dirt and debris in existing ducts, voids, etc. Advise planning supervisor on pre-qualification requirements of potential specialist contractors.                                          P

#### *Hazardous materials/substances*

All major service sizes and routes to be arranged to minimise cutting and chasing, where reasonably practicable, thereby avoiding or minimising dust and noise hazards. Take advantage of the requirement for a smaller lift shaft (from existing bed lift to new passenger lift) to accommodate a vertical riser for services, noting that separation will be needed to ensure safe access to the service duct and to comply with the standard requirements for lift shaft design.    P

Position new service runs in ceiling voids and partition/dry lining insulation cavities, taking adequate measures to ensure safe access provisions for maintenance and adequate protection of services. The integrity of fire compartmentation must be considered when determining service runs, and any penetrations detailed appropriately.    F

Consideration to be given to connection of new piped services. Off-site prefabrication and the use of threaded/compression connections will minimise hot-working fire/explosion hazards, particularly in areas of existing buildings with combustible materials and high dust concentrations, i.e. timber and roof spaces. These risks must be weighed against the increased risk of leaks causing hazards, such as damage to electrical installations or increased requirements for potential repair.    P/F

Consider all materials being incorporated into the services design and flag all potentially hazardous materials or substances which cannot reasonably be avoided in the health and safety plan, i.e. connections to existing painted pipework.    P/F

Identify combustible materials and substances which cannot be reasonably avoided, e.g. bottled gas for cutting and welding.    P/F

Consider methods of fixing new services and plant to existing structure to avoid or minimise the creation of dust, chemical, or physical hazards, where possible.    P

The specification must set out requirements for the capping and temporary sealing of all pipework and ductwork, in storage and as soon as practicable during installation, to avoid the ingress of dust and other contamination which could create health and safety hazards for commissioning engineers and the end user.    P

### Programme

The programme requirements for the engineering services installation should be reviewed with the planning supervisor.    P

### *Review all health and safety hazards relating to the maintenance, cleaning, repair, replacement, decommissioning, dismantling or removal of the engineering plant, equipment and services installations*

### Access

Consider layout of all items of plant and equipment in new boiler house/plant room, ensuring that adequate space is available for ease of maintenance without risk to the health and safety of maintenance operatives.

Boiler plant is to be designed with a suitable flue system located to minimise future maintenance and repair risks, and to provide hazard free outlet arrangements.    F

The cistern installation in the roof space will be designed with stair access from stair 1 and a cat ladder emergency escape into stair 2. Kitchen air handling plant to be accessed from kitchen directly into roof space local to equipment. Adequate areas around the cisterns and equipment, together with walkways, will be boarded out and guarded to prevent falls through fragile ceilings.    F

Improved access to the existing lift motor room will be incorporated with the new roof space tank room access. Adequate lighting, including emergency lighting, ventilation, fire detection and alarm systems will be provided in the lift motor room and roof plant spaces, taking into account the possibility of lone working.                                                                                          F

New riser duct adjacent to lift will be provided with full platforms at each floor level to prevent falls, and with adequate lighting arrangements. Isolation valves and electrical isolators will be clearly identified outside the duct housing.                                                                              F

Certain ceiling mounted equipment will require the use of temporary staging to facilitate maintenance, repair, etc., e.g. fan coil units, small comfort cooling units, and so on.                                      F

The locations of all service runs, light fittings, valves, control panels, fire dampers, smoke detectors, etc. will be determined to ensure their accessibility and security. Walkways and crawlways with adequate lighting provisions will be incorporated into roof space.                                 F

### Isolation

Adequate isolation provisions, including lock-off systems where appropriate, for plant, equipment and service runs to be incorporated into details/specification to allow for safe maintenance, e.g. valves, drain taps, vents, local electrical isolators. Provisions to be documented in health and safety file.                                                                                                              F

### Lifting requirements

Incorporate lifting beams, brackets and eyes to ensure that large or heavy items of plant and equipment can be lifted and moved where such a requirement can be reasonably foreseen, e.g. lift motor room, boiler house.                                                                                       F

### Maintenance procedures

Specification to include requirements for all maintenance and cleaning procedures to be clearly documented by plant and equipment manufacturers/suppliers.                                                      F

Low maintenance plant and equipment to be specified for areas where access for maintenance will require special provisions, i.e. high level external lighting, cctv cameras.                                      F

### Hazardous materials/substances

Avoid any potentially harmful or combustible materials or substances where reasonably practicable or use less hazardous alternatives, i.e. use nickel cadmium batteries not lead acid ones for emergency lighting and alarm systems. Flag any harmful or combustible materials or substances which are incorporated.                                                                                          P/F

Secure rooms/cupboards for the storage of any potentially hazardous maintenance materials or substances, e.g. water treatment chemicals, lubricants, cleaning substances, etc. are to be provided and designed to meet manufacturers' requirements (e.g. for ventilation).                                     F

### Identification

Specify markings, labelling and signing requirements for all service runs, plant and equipment to ensure that they are clearly identifiable.                                                                        F

### Re-assessment of the health and safety knowledge boundary

The engineering services designer's knowledge remains adequate.

Contractors familiar with stripping out potentially hazardous materials and with purging existing services to be covered by prequalification requirements. Contractors will be required to prove their competence and the adequacy of their resources.

*Action required*

Health and safety issues are to be recorded in the health and safety plan to ensure consideration by contractors prior to and during the construction process. Any information for inclusion in the health and safety file should be logged and stored where necessary.

Discuss any health and safety matters arising out of the issues considered to date with the planning supervisor, highlighting those which affect other designers.

## 7.6 THE BUILDING SERVICES ENGINEER'S CONTRIBUTION TO THE PRE-TENDER STAGE HEALTH AND SAFETY PLAN*

Sections to be amplified are shown in square brackets [..].

### 1. General

[*Introduction by planning supervisor, setting out objective of the plan and the obligations of the principal contractor in relation to development of the plan*].

### 2. Nature of project

[*Name of client and location of work will be specified by planning supervisor*].

The construction work:

> [*General description of work by planning supervisor, together with, or incorporating brief elemental descriptions provided by all design consultants*]

Services stripping-out work:

> **The following existing services, plant and equipment are to be removed: [List]**
>
> **The following existing services, plant and equipment are to be retained and adequately protected: [List]**

Engineering services work:

- **disposal systems - alteration and extension of existing above ground drainage**
- **piped supply systems - installation of new hot and cold water services, and gas; refurbishment of existing hydrant and hose reel systems**
- **mechanical heating/cooling/refrigeration systems - installation of new heating system**
- **ventilation/air conditioning systems - installation of new unitised bathroom/toilet extract ventilation and kitchen ventilation**
- **electrical supply/power/lighting - alteration and extension of existing internal power and lighting systems and the installation of new external lighting**

---

* In this example plan, the case study designer's inputs to the plan are shown in bold face, while the inputs of others are shown in italics.

- communication/security/control systems - the installation of new fire detection and alarm systems, telephone, tv and cctv services, and call system
- transport systems - refurbishment of existing lift installation.

Timescale for completion of construction:

> **The proposed overall timescale for construction, including stripping out and commissioning, is nine months.**
>
> **In preparing the detailed programme for the works, the activities of different engineering trade contractors must be co-ordinated and rationalised.**
>
> **Adequate allowance must be made in the programming of the works for the purging of services, the removal of asbestos by a specialist contractor and the provision of safe working procedures for all hazardous operations.**
> *[Additional input by other designers and planning supervisor as necessary].*

## 3.     The existing environment

Surrounding land uses and related restrictions:

*[Contractors to take steps to minimise noise from plant and equipment during construction].*

### Existing services:

**There are no overhead services.**

**Original record drawings, together with survey drawings, showing underground services and layout of existing internal services are included in the tender documents. The contractor is to employ pipe/cable locating equipment to establish the precise routing of all underground services in the vicinity of any excavation works before work begins.**

**The contractor is to establish formal procedures to ensure that any unidentified services located during the works are carefully checked to determine if they are live or contain any hazardous materials or substances. All details must be recorded. The services engineer and planning supervisor are to be provided with copies of the records setting out the nature and location of all such services prior to the agreement of a course of action.**

**The purging of existing pipework will be necessary prior to stripping out or alteration to eliminate the risks from any potentially hazardous substances. The contractor must establish procedures for the safe disposal of purge effluent.**

**Painted and galvanised pipework and tanks exist which will require care to avoid creating toxic fumes when these are removed, altered or extended.**

### Existing traffic systems and restrictions:

*[General information and restrictions to be set out by planning supervisor].*

**A schedule of plant and equipment sizes for delivery to site is included in the tender documents.**

### Existing buildings:

**A health clearance certificate for the buildings has been issued by Health Authority.**

**Investigations have revealed asbestos insulation in basement, painted and galvanised**

pipework and tanks, pcbs in light fittings and fluorescent lighting tubes.

The location and extent of the known hazardous substances and materials are shown on drawings incorporated in the tender documents.

Consideration must be given to the health and safety of all persons entering the existing buildings prior to, or during construction, so that they are aware of and protected from any potentially harmful substances and materials.

Tests for gases (e.g. $CO_2$, methane, etc.) should be carried out for all confined spaces and ducts.

Dust, dirt, other debris and possibly vermin should be expected in service ducts and floor, ceiling or roof voids. Appropriate control measures during stripping out and cleaning will be required.

*[Further information provided by other designers as necessary].*

### *Ground conditions:*

*[Sufficient ground investigation data to be provided to ensure that adequate measures are taken during construction to prevent or reduce risks to workers from collapse of excavations, contamination or contact with live services during underground service alterations].*

## 4.      Existing drawings

Available record drawings and survey information in relation to existing services both in the buildings and externally above and below ground form part of the tender documents. *[Additional record information to be provided by other designers].*

## 5.      The design

Hazards and work sequences have been identified during the design which are likely to pose a risk to the health and safety of construction workers, but cannot be avoided. These are divided into two categories:

(a) where standard solutions apply which will minimise and/or control the risks
(b) where special solutions will be required.

It should be noted, however, that standard solutions are not free from risks and that appropriate measures must be taken by contractors to minimise and/or control the risks.

This list does not include common place site hazards which must be controlled by the application of normal good site management practices.

A  General:
• Work at high level (a)
• Temporary lighting, power and other supplies (a)
*[Other designers' input]*

C  Stripping Out (demolition):
• Removal of asbestos (b)
• Removal of painted and galvanised pipework and cisterns (b)
• Removal of lead pipework (b)
• Purging and removal of pipework containing potentially hazardous substances (b)
• Removal of existing ductwork which may contain hazardous material (b)

- Control of dust, dirt and other debris in ducts, floor, ceiling and roof voids (a)
- Removal of lighting fittings with pcbs and fluorescent tubes (a)
- Work in confined spaces (a).

[*Other designers' input*]

**D  Groundworks:**
- Identification of existing underground service routes (a)
- Stability of excavations (a).

[*Other designers' input*]

**R  Disposal Systems:**
- Method of fixing to existing structure (a)
- Connection to existing, possibly contaminated, underground drainage (b).

[*Other designers' input*]

**S  Piped Supply Systems:**
- Alteration/extension of painted and galvanised pipework (b)
- Alteration and extension of pipework containing potentially hazardous substances (b)
- Access for installation of cisterns, calorifiers, etc. (b)
- Method of fixing to existing structure (a)
- Methods of flushing, cleaning, pressure testing, chlorination and commissioning (a).

**T  Mechanical Heating/Cooling/Refrigeration Systems:**
- Access for installation of major items of plant and equipment (b)
- Gas boiler installation (a)
- Method of fixing to existing structure (a)
- Methods of commissioning (a).

**U  Ventilation/Air Conditioning Systems:**
- Access for installation of major items of plant and equipment (b)
- Method of fixing to existing structure (a)
- Methods of cleaning and commissioning (a).

**V  Electrical Supply/Power/Lighting Systems:**
- Compliance with IEE regulations (a)
- Electrical isolation (b)
- Installation of high level external lighting (a)
- Method of fixing to existing structure (a)
- Method of testing and commissioning (a).

**W  Communications/Security/Control Systems:**
- Installation of high level external cameras (a)
- Method of fixing to existing structure (a)
- Method of testing and commissioning (a).

[*Other work sections'/ designers' input*].

The design assumes the following work/assembly sequences to reduce the health and safety risks to construction workers:

- all asbestos being removed (by a licensed contractor) and the existing piped services purged prior to the commencement of general stripping out or other construction work
- the removal of dust, dirt and other debris from service ducts and floor, ceiling and roof voids prior to the commencement of the new installations
- the existing hose reel system being available for fire protection use during construction
- access improvements being incorporated to ease removal of existing cisterns in roof space, basement plant and other large items of plant and equipment.

[*Any other specific sequences of work or assembly specified by other designers*].

Specific activities requiring contractors to prepare detailed method statements for managing those aspects of the work will be:

- asbestos removal (showing compliance with asbestos regulations)
- purging of existing services, including safe disposal of effluent
- stripping out, dismantling and disposal of existing services, plant and equipment
- provision of temporary lighting, power and other supplies
- installation of major items of plant and equipment
- refurbishment/alteration of existing lift car and shaft
- fixing methods for services, plant and equipment
- fire precautions for hot working methods
- capping and temporary sealing of pipelines and ductwork
- testing, flushing and chemical cleaning/treatment of services
- commissioning.

[*Other activities identified by other designers*].

## 6. Construction materials

The following potentially hazardous construction materials and substances are required by the design:

- the need to use bottled gas during construction for cutting and welding
- refrigerants
- the use of water treatment chemicals during pre-commissioning cleaning.

[*Other hazardous materials and substances required by other designers*].

The contractor is required to take appropriate measures to control the risks created by these hazards, to explain the proposed measures in his tender and to prepare detailed method statements for managing these aspects of the works.

Other common materials and substances used during construction will also present health and/or safety hazards, requiring the contractor to carry out COSHH or other risk assessments and to introduce control measures. These are deemed to be within the normal experience of a competent contractor and have not, therefore, been listed here.

## 7. Site wide elements

Unloading and/or storage facilities will be required for the following plant and equipment:

- boilers, calorifiers and cisterns
- air handling units
- pipework and radiators
- control panels, conduit and cable trays.

[*Unloading/storage facilities specified by other designers*].

Suitable safe storage will also be required for bottled gases.

## 8. Overlap with client's undertaking

The client will commence occupation of the premises one week prior to the completion of commissioning. All O & M manuals and 'as installed' drawings must be available in advance of this time.

## 9.     Site Rules

The principal contractor's site rules must include his provisions for:

- restriction of access during asbestos removal, until clearance certificate issued
- conformity with all statutory requirements, including electricity at work, PPE at work, COSHH, noise at work, etc. regulations
- hot-working and confined space 'permit to work' system required complying with appropriate HSE and other recommendations
- strict control whilst client in occupation and during commissioning, in respect of contractor's access, opening up of ceilings, ducts, plant rooms, control panels, etc. and working on live systems
- a formal reporting system for unforeseen eventualities.

[*Any other rules required by client, planning supervisor or other designers*]

## 10.     Continuing liaison

The procedures for the consideration and acceptability of the health and safety implications of contractor design elements of the work must follow the recognised principles of prevention and protection and take into account issues highlighted in the pre-tender stage health and safety plan. The details of health or safety issues, risk assessments and hazards which cannot be designed out are to be submitted to the planning supervisor, together with the proposals for mitigation or control measures required during construction, maintenance, repair, replacement, dismantling and disposal. All such information is to be submitted in sufficient time to allow adequate consideration by the planning supervisor and, where appropriate, the design consultants.

The following action is to be taken in the event of unforeseen eventualities arising during construction which require significant design changes or affect the resources required:

- the planning supervisor is to be advised as soon as possible
- details of the health and safety issues of the eventuality are to be submitted to the planning supervisor as soon as possible
- details of the re-design and its health and safety implications are to be submitted to planning supervisor for consideration and agreement in sufficient time to allow adequate consultation prior to the execution of the affected works.

## 7.7    THE HEALTH AND SAFETY FILE (ENGINEERING SERVICES)

### *Concept decisions*

The alternatives of refurbishment, or demolition and rebuilding have been compared. Having considered the balance of health and safety risks in these two alternatives, together with meeting the client's objectives, aesthetics and buildability, against the relative costs, including those of potential accidents, delays, etc. resulting from health and safety incidents, it has been decided to proceed on the basis of refurbishment. Significant hazards remain which will need to be assessed carefully by the designer during the development of the design to try to avoid or, where this is not possible, to reduce the risks to the health and safety of all those involved in maintenance, repair and eventual dismantling or demolition of the works.

### Design criteria

The following criteria were used in the design of the building services installations:

[List all relevant design data, regulations used in design, etc.]

### Existing record/survey information

The following existing services record drawings and survey drawings form part of this health and safety file:

[List relevant drawings]

### Construction methods

Sectional boilers and cisterns have been used to reduce manual handling risks.

Off-site pre-fabrication together with the use of threaded fittings for all new steel pipework up to 2" dia. within the existing building to minimise the need for hot-working methods. Steel pipework $2^1/2$" dia. and above has welded connections.

The integrity of fire compartmentation where service runs pass through fire compartment walls must be maintained.

### Construction materials

The following hazardous materials and substances are incorporated/inherent in the building services installation:

[List, e.g. water treatment chemicals, lubricants, refrigerants, etc.]

### Details of equipment and maintenance facilities

The following provisions have been incorporated into the project to avoid or reduce health and safety risks associated with the maintenance and repair of the building services:

[List, e.g. access arrangements, lifting facilities, lighting provisions, storage of hazardous substances, etc.]

The following test certificates are provided in relation to the building services installation:

[List, e.g. motors, pressure vessels, electrical distribution system, pipework systems, etc.]

### Maintenance procedures and requirements

The following procedures should be followed for the safe maintenance of the building services:

[List, e.g. permit to work system for hot-working, electrical work, etc.; testing and maintenance of lifting and access equipment, all other general maintenance procedures/requirements not covered in O & M manuals]

Reference must also be made to the maintenance procedures and requirements set out in the O & M manuals.

### Plant and equipment schedules and O & M manuals

The following plant and equipment schedules are appended:

[List]

The following operation and maintenance manuals form part of this health and safety file:

[List]

### Location and identification of services and utilities

In addition to the existing record drawings and survey drawings noted before, the following 'as installed' drawings for the services and utilities form part of this health and safety file:

[List]

The services, plant and equipment markings, labelling and signing designations are as laid out in the O & M manuals and on the 'as installed' drawings.

# 8 Building superstructure

## 8.1 INTRODUCTION

This example describes the approach adopted by the structural designer of a major retail development, which includes a filling station and surface car park. It is based on a real situation, although some aspects have been simplified for the sake of clarity.

The design is progressed through three stages:

- concept
- outline
- detailed.

## 8.2 PROJECT INFORMATION

### 8.2.1 Client requirements

The client, from market research, perceives an opportunity to develop a large out-of-town food superstore with good road access from adjacent residential areas. Adequate land area for a single storey superstore of approximately 6,500 square metres, a filling station and parking for 800 vehicles is required.

To provide flexibility of operations, only three internal columns are permitted within the actual sales floor area of 4,700 square metres. Column spacing within ancillary areas is not so critical.

Closed circuit television surveillance of the site, including car parking areas, is to be provided.

The business park already has planning permission for retail development on this part of the site and the road access and population catchment area meet the client's requirements.

The budget for the project, excluding the cost of land, is £8.5M.

### 8.2.2 Project status

The project on which this example is based was complete and the superstore successfully trading before this report was drafted. The author, whilst having no direct involvement in the project, was aware of its progress and, on occasions, was asked for structural advice by the project engineer.

The design team, which comprised an architect, a structural/civil engineer and a building services engineer, were well known to each other, having worked together on several previous occasions.

The contract route was one that is becoming increasingly common, i.e. the design team was initially appointed by the client - the end user, and their contracts were taken over by the contractor, when appointed, under a 'Design and Build' contract. This arrangement worked well.

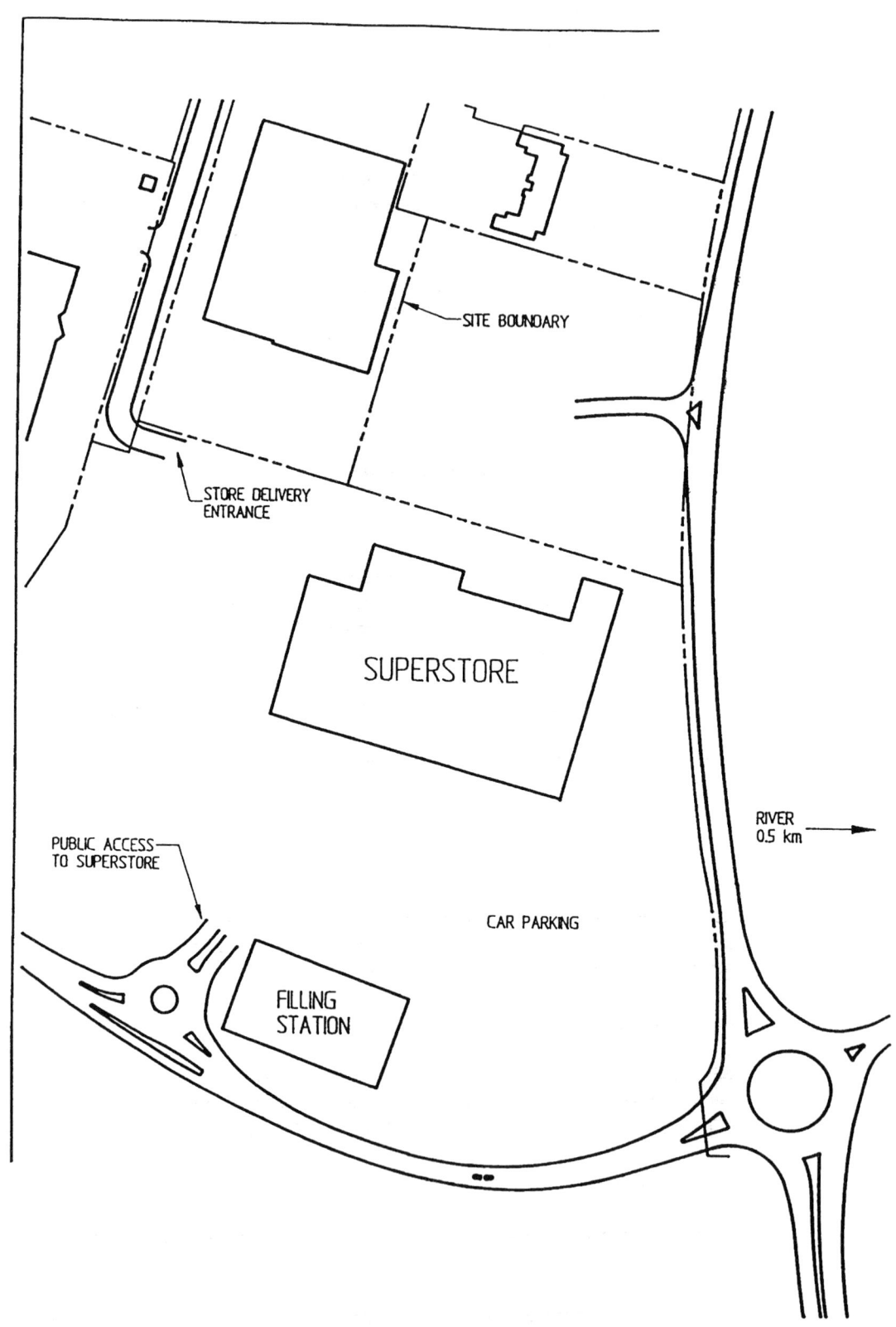

**Figure 11** *Superstore site layout*

### 8.2.3    Local environment

The selected site is part of a retail/business park situated in the flood plain of a non-tidal river which bisects the park. The retail site is not immediately adjacent to the river, but the possibility of flooding both during construction and when the store is in operation will have to be verified. The existing site ground levels render the area subject to flooding with a 1 in 50 year return period.

The site was previously occupied by an aircraft factory which included a foundry; the likelihood of contaminants being found on the site is, therefore, high.

### 8.2.4    Site layout

The site layout showing the possible positioning of the store, the filling station, the car parking areas and the road access is shown in Figure 11.

## 8.3    CONCEPT DESIGN STAGE

### 8.3.1    Discussion of health and safety issues

'F' in the right-hand margin denotes an item which should be incorporated in the project file and 'P' an item to be included in the plan.

#### *Primary health and safety issues*

There are three issues:

- possibility of contaminated land due to previous site usage (aircraft factory)
- non-tidal river, liable to flooding
- pollution of river from site storage of petroleum spirits and lorry wash-down area.

#### *Identification of principal hazards for construction*

The principal hazards are thought to be:

- removal of possible ground contamination
- fire/explosion of petroleum spirits
- site access (until the permanent road re-alignment has been carried out)
- risk of flooding and high water table (for excavations)
- steel frame erection.

#### *Initial assessment of the strategic issues*

- 'specialist' contractors will need to be appointed if ground contamination is subsequently confirmed by a site investigation

- it is also recognised that the development must comply with the Petroleum Regulations and that the close co-operation of the local Fire Officer will be essential.

#### *Review of possible design solutions*

The risk of flooding is unacceptable to the client who accepts the cost consequences of raising the ground floor of the development to a level that will ensure it is above that reached by a 1 in 200 year return flood. To cater for this, flood detention storage will be required to maintain the existing storage volume available to the river on the flood plain. The car park provides one possible means of achieving this, and the client accepts the probability that car parking areas could be subject to periodic flooding.

Surface water drainage systems must incorporate interceptors to avoid pollution of the river. These will have to be regularly maintained by the client.

If a site investigation reveals the presence of contaminated land, all such material will be treated.

### 8.3.2    Designer's contribution to the health and safety plan and file

The health and safety issues identified at the concept design stage which will need consideration by the designer for the plan and file are listed below.

*The river*

The surrounding area is low lying and within the flood plain, as defined by the National Rivers Authority, of the non-tidal river which bisects the business park. The water table is likely to be within 1-2 metres of the flood plain surface; this will be confirmed by a site investigation.          P/F

*The site*

Contaminated ground may also be present; this will be confirmed by the site investigation.

The site may contain existing foundations as well as uncharted cables and services.          P/F

*Storage of fuel*

The risk of fire and explosion from the site storage of petroleum spirit must be recognised at the outline and detailed design stages. Pollution from accidental spillage of fuel must be prevented.          P/F

*Consideration at the outline design stage*

It is recommended that:

*   measures to protect buildings against flooding are adopted          F

*   measures to prevent pollution of the river are adopted          F

*   a full site investigation is carried out to determine geotechnical parameters, possible ground contamination and the location of any existing underground services or foundations          P/F

*   measures to protect the works against flooding during construction are also adopted.          P

## 8.4    OUTLINE DESIGN STAGE

### 8.4.1    Discussion of health and safety issues

*Examination of design options*

In practice, design options available for the superstructure of the proposed 'superstore' are limited to steel and concrete. Either could be adopted as neither offers any advantage as regards general health and safety issues. However, owing to the client's requirement for a large span, minimum column environment, steel is the most suitable solution.

For foundations, the options available include piling, raft, and mass concrete footings. The site is not close to residential areas and therefore, should piling be necessary, the question of noise will not be a problem. The use of bored piling could, however, pose risks to the site operatives, if the ground is contaminated. Based on the findings of the site investigation, the preferred solution for the foundation is for mass concrete footings with a ground bearing floor slab. This solution does not impose any extra risks to those carrying out the construction, other than those normally expected and managed by competent contractors on construction sites.

### Principles for design of structural elements

The following principles were considered and adopted at the outline design stage:

- utilise prefabricated steel assemblies wherever possible to reduce work at height

- specify all steelwork to be blast cleaned and painted in the fabrication works to reduce access requirements at site and the risks associated with handling 'rusting' steel, i.e. dust

- position heavy plant at ground level rather than at roof level, if space permits

- provide a safe access for cleaning the roof atria, both internally and externally. This may be achieved by ensuring that all access ladders and external roof walkways are equipped with safety hoops and handrails, and that hooks for the attachment of safety harnesses are provided on the atria structure. Internally, the atria is likely to be cleaned using 'cherry pickers'; these will require adequate operating space

- non-fragile roof coverings will be specified

- wherever possible, reduce the need for access to internal gutters by arranging roof slopes to drain to the building perimeter.

### Hazards arising from structural design decisions

Road transport regulations limit the maximum length of items which can be transported without making special arrangements with the police and other appropriate authorities. The length of steel roof beams required to provide the client with the specified clear span criteria will prevent their being shop assembled and transported as a single member.

Site erection of structural steel is a hazardous operation; the use of experienced steel erectors will reduce the risks, although it should be recognised that these cannot be eliminated altogether. Lifts will be heavy and the contractor should be alerted to the low bearing capacity of the ground and provide a method statement which will include ensuring the stability of cranes.

Bolting up of roof lattice girders will be carried out at ground level and adequate space for site assembly will be required together with the necessary erection plant, i.e. mobile cranes, assembly jigs, temporary bracing.

Wherever possible, bolted connections will be used to avoid the need for extensive site welding. Where this is unavoidable, it will be carried out in accordance with approved guidance and regulations. Any damaged area of paint will need to be 'touched up' on site; both the shop applied and any site touch-up paint will be applied strictly in accordance with the manufacturers' recommendations. A safe system of access for site touch-up painting will be agreed before any work is carried out.

Generally, decisions concerning the structure were made by the structural engineer, although these were always discussed with the architect and the building services engineer when there was any likelihood of conflict over detail. This was particularly important over issues which had an impact on visual aspects of the project.

*Roofs*

Cleaning of the roof atria will entail operatives gaining access to the roof area; provision must be made for the securing of safety harnesses during cleaning operations.

### Hazards that have not been eliminated

The following non-structural hazards have not been eliminated at this stage, but will need to be considered subsequently:

- site access during construction

- flooding of works during construction

- contaminated land (the site investigation has confirmed the existence of 'heavy' metals)

- petroleum spirit (storage and spillage).

## 8.4.2   Designer's contribution to the health and safety plan and file

The health and safety issues identified at the outline design stage which will need consideration by the designer for the plan and file are listed below.

### The structure

Erection of structural steel is a hazardous operation. The design should be as simple as possible, using bolted connections wherever appropriate. Connections should be simply supported. Roof lattice girders should be pre-assembled in the workshop in as large a section as road transport regulations permit. Site assembly of sections should be carried out at ground level to avoid working at height. Alert the contractor to the low bearing capacity of the ground and the effect on crane stability.                                                                                                  P

Specifications should ensure that structural steel members are blast cleaned and painted before delivery to site.                                                                                                                              P

Roof slopes will be arranged to drain to the building perimeter. This will avoid access to internal gutters and the potential for water penetration within the retail store.                                       P

### Maintenance access

Safe access for cleaning of roof glazing must be provided, as must provision for securing of safety harnesses for maintenance personnel.                                                                                P/F

### Roof covering

With the obvious exception of the glazed atria, non-fragile roof coverings will be specified, thereby reducing the risk of falls during maintenance.                                                                      P/F

## 8.5 DETAILED DESIGN STAGE

### 8.5.1 Discussion of health and safety issues

*Examination of structural design options*

At this stage, the design strategy has been resolved and it is necessary to consider means of reducing the hazards that have been identified.

Framing of the building superstructure will be of structural steel, with long span latticed roof beams. These will be pre-assembled at the fabrication works into as large a section as permitted by road transport regulations.

Roof cladding will be a steel deck with a sheet waterproof membrane, thereby avoiding the risks associated with asphalt waterproofing. Side cladding will be of cavity brickwork containing traditional shop windows.

The design solution for the foundations will utilise mass concrete footings to the columns with strip footings for the perimeter walls and a ground bearing floor slab.

*Review design details for each work section*

*Excavation*

Following a decision to remove all contaminated ground from the site, no specific risks to the health and safety of the subsequent construction workforce are expected from this aspect.

Ground conditions are generally good, and excavations for footings are not expected to be so deep as to require shoring. Care will, however, be necessary where local depths of excavation extend below the water table. In these circumstances, pumping of groundwater and shoring may be necessary.

*Frame Erection*

Wherever possible, site connections for the structural steel frame will be bolted to avoid the risks associated with site welding. Where site welding is necessary, weld procedures and welder qualifications will be required before any welding is carried out. The steelwork contractor will be required to provide holes in structural members suitable for the attachment of erectors' safety harnesses. The location and extent of these will be the responsibility of the fabricator.

Secondary steelwork will be minimal, being used only as head restraint for the external brickwork and around openings through the roof deck.

*Review construction method sequences and programme*

Stability of the structural frame will be an important element of the erection phase. Structural stability of the completed building will be provided by vertical bracing in the plane of the walls in those bays which will accommodate brickwork. Temporary bracing of the partially erected structure will be required until sufficient permanent bracing has been installed. Suggested temporary bracing will be shown on the contract drawings together with member loads. The steelwork erector will be expected to consider this and demonstrate adequate provision in his method statement.

During erection of the structural frame and roof covering, no other work shall be permitted within the curtilage of the area being erected. The contractor should be advised so that his programme can accommodate this.

It is expected that the structure will be erected progressively from the south east corner, working across the site in a north westerly direction. Areas which have been lined and levelled and finally bolted up and all roof cladding completed may be released for access by following trades.

### Maintenance and repair strategy for each work section

Thanks to the controlled environment, routine maintenance of the structural frame should not be necessary.

The roof atria will, however, have to be cleaned and a safe system of work is required. Access for the external cleaning will be provided by fixed ladders to the general roof area, and then by dedicated roof walkways to the perimeter of the atria. All vertical ladders will be provided with safety hoops, roof walkways with handrails on both sides and the atria structure with a safety rail to its perimeter for the attachment of safety harnesses.

Access for the cleaning of the internal surfaces of the atria glazing will be achieved using 'cherry pickers'. This will only be carried out when the store is closed to avoid risks to staff and the public.

### Demolition strategy

Demolition is not envisaged to cause specific problems. Roof and vertical cladding may be dismantled by removing the bolted fixings. The steel frame may be dismantled by reversing the erection procedures. Temporary bracing will be needed in the event of dismantling.

Specialist advice will be necessary when removing filling station storage tanks; this will be done in accordance with the Petroleum Regulations.


## 8.6   THE STRUCTURAL ENGINEER'S CONTRIBUTION TO THE PRE-TENDER STAGE HEALTH AND SAFETY PLAN*


## 1.      Nature of project

| | |
|---|---|
| Name of client: | *A supermarket chain* |
| Location: | *Retail/Business Park, at (address)* |
| The construction work: | **The work entails the construction of a single storey steel framed retail superstore, a petrol filling station and car parking for 800 vehicles.** |
| | **Foundations are of mass concrete footings with the ground floor slab, ground bearing.** |
| | **As the building is to be sited in the river flood plain, the floor level of the building will be raised to reduce the risk of flooding.** |

---

\* In this example plan, the case study designer's inputs to the plan are shown in bold face, while the inputs of others are shown in italics.

Timescale for completion
of construction work:     *The construction period will be 44 weeks. Trading to commence
                          within 16 months from granting of planning permission.*

Note: A schedule of the relevant drawings is at Annex A (actual drawings not included in case study).

## 2.     The existing environment

*The site is situated on a retail/business park of 300 acres which was formerly the site of an aircraft factory. The area on which the retail superstore is to be built is situated in the flood plain of a non-tidal river which bisects the business park. The site is not immediately adjacent to the river, and therefore problems associated with working over or adjacent to water will not apply. Full detailed planning approval has been granted but with the following restrictions on construction activities:*

- *although residential properties are some 100 metres away, weekend working will not be permitted*
- *noise levels from construction work will be kept to a minimum at all times and not exceed 85Db(a) between the hours of 8.00pm and 7.00am*
- *the entire site will be securely fenced to prevent access by children.*

*Ground contamination in the form of 'heavy' metals has been identified, arising from previous site usage. All such material will be removed by specialists, as part of the main contract, before any general construction work commences.*

*Existing foundations have also been identified on the site, although the presence of underground services has not. (Site Plan x)*

*The site access will be from High Street; attention should be paid to the existing limited visibility due to inadequate sight lines until the road diversions, to be carried out by the Local Authority, have been completed.*

**Ground conditions are generally good and shoring of excavations for mass concrete footings is not envisaged. For other excavations, and particularly those below the level of the site water table (1.5 metres below existing ground level), special measures will be required. This will apply in particular to the installation of petrol interceptors and fuel storage tanks for the filling station.**

## 3.     Existing drawings

*Details of the buildings which previously occupied the site are shown on Drawing X . These may be of use in determining the likely location of existing foundations.*

*Also included are drawings of the river and its associated flood plain area (Drawings Y and Z.)*

## 4.     The design

### *Retail Building*

**The structural steel frame will derive its overall stability from horizontal bracing in the plane of the roof, the reaction forces of which are resisted by vertical bracing in designated bays of the perimeter walls. Until the structure has been lined and levelled and all bracing securely fixed, temporary bracing will be required. The steel erector's method statement should take this into account.**

Due to the limitation on the length of structural members which may be transported by road, it will be necessary to site join those sections of roof lattice girders previously assembled in the fabricator's works. Adequate space and lifting equipment must be made available to enable this to be carried out safely.

During steel erection and fixing of roof cladding, no following trade shall be permitted access to the area of building being erected.

All steelwork will be shot blasted and painted at the works, with any damaged areas of paint being 'touched up' on site after erection. Safe means of access will be required to enable this painting to be carried out.

Wherever possible, all site connections of steelwork will be bolted to avoid the risks associated with welding. Site welding shall only be permitted following approval of welding procedures and by qualified welders.

All beam to column connections shall be 'simple'. All main structural members shall be provided with safety holes for the attachment of safety harnesses by those carrying out work on the structure.

Maintenance access to the roof shall be provided by vertical ladders; all ladders will have safety hoops and lockable gates at the base to prevent unauthorised access. All roof access walkways, as shown on the contract drawings, shall have safety handrails each side.

Cleaning of the roof atria is a potentially hazardous operation; provision must be made for the securing of safety harnesses during such operations. Details of such a system are shown on the contract drawings. The contractors' attention is drawn to this matter as it will affect their carrying out of the works.

*(Note: Other designers will also have an input to this plan, i.e. architects, services engineers).*

### The Filling Station

The kiosk is of traditional brick construction and the forecourt canopy is framed in structural steelwork. The filling station will be operational in advance of the retail unit and, as large quantities of petroleum spirits will be stored on the site, a real risk of fire/explosion exists. The contractor shall ensure that all construction work is carried out in accordance with the Petroleum Regulations and that full co-operation is afforded the local Fire Officer. Strict site rules regarding 'No Smoking' or 'Naked Lights' shall be enforced.

All drainage systems from the filling station forecourt must incorporate petrol interceptors to prevent pollution of the river.

Due to the high site water table, all interceptors and underground fuel storage tanks must be 'tied down' during the placing of encasement concrete (the local Fire Officer will not permit encasement other than in concrete) to prevent floatation. All excavations for interceptors and fuel tanks will require dewatering and sides will need support.

### Car Park

*The car park area is to be designed with proper drainage falls. In order to compensate for the raising of the floor level of the retail building, it can be designed to act as a detention basin in time of severe storm. In order to minimise pollution of the river, the surface water drainage from the car park area must pass to a settlement chamber.*

## 5. Construction materials

**The following health hazards from materials have been identified which cannot be avoided and which will demand precautions to safeguard the health of construction workers:**

**Stanchions - Epoxy grout for holding down bolts.**

*(Note: information on other materials in this section will be provided by other designers).*

## 6 Site wide elements

*The following hazards have been identified which cannot be avoided and which will be a risk to the safety of construction workers:*

- *site access and egress throughout construction and especially after the petrol filling station has been handed over to the client*

- *access for lifting crane for roof girders*

- *groundwater table and its effect on excavations*

- **erection area for the site jointing of roof lattice girders**

- **stability of large span lattice girders until permanently braced and bolted down.**

## 7. Overlap with client's undertaking

*The client has no ongoing operation on the site and therefore there is no health and safety implication to the works from his activities. Once the petrol filling station has been handed over, site traffic must be controlled to ensure that the interface with public traffic does not cause risks to public safety.*

## 8. Site Rules

*The contractor is reminded of the high public profile which the client enjoys and shall therefore ensure that no site activity reflects adversely on the client.*

*The following rules have been devised to control the risks arising from the identified hazards:*

- *no smoking or naked lights within 20 metres of the area of the filling station*

- *all site operatives to undergo a site safety induction course before commencing work on site*

- *no general construction work shall commence until the resident engineer is satisfied that all contaminated material has been removed from site*

- *access roads and footpaths must be kept free from spoil and debris at all times*

- *rubbish shall be regularly removed to an authorised tip.*

## 9.    Continuing liaison

*The following procedures shall be adopted for the consideration and acceptance of the health and safety implications of design elements of the principal contractor and other contractors' packages:*

- *details of the health and safety issues shall be submitted to the planning supervisor, including the results of appropriate risk assessments*

- *the implications arising from the design of temporary works shall be submitted in sufficient time before they are due to commence to allow for full consideration.*

*Procedures for dealing with unforeseen events during the project which result in substantial design changes and which might affect resources are as follows:*

- *in the event of any unforeseen circumstance, the planning supervisor is to be informed immediately by the principal contractor*

- *the health and safety issues arising from any unforeseen occurrence are to be submitted to the planning supervisor as soon as is possible after the event*

- *in the event that any re-design is required, for whatever reason, the health and safety implications are to be submitted for consideration and acceptance by the planning supervisor in due time before execution.*

Note:  The following section is not required by the Approved Code of Practice although for completeness it is recommended that, where appropriate, it should be included.

## 10.    Method statements

**The preferred contractor (or short-listed contractors) will be required to present and justify method statements to the post tender examination board for the following work sequences:**

**[List of operations]**

## Annex A

**Schedule of relevant drawings**
(drawings not included in case study).

## 8.7    THE HEALTH AND SAFETY FILE

Within the Approved Code of Practice (ACOP), Appendix 5 provides guidance on what should be included within the health and safety file.  For this particular project/example, the file should contain:

- copies of all general arrangement and detail drawings produced by the design team, including 'as built' drawings where appropriate, and details of the design criteria, i.e. design loading

- details of the materials used in the permanent works together with method statements of how the building was constructed

- details of maintenance procedures for the structure, i.e. requirements for painting of exposed steelwork, access to, and cleaning of, atria, gutters etc.

• details of maintenance of petrol/oil interceptors

• technical details of any equipment installed within or on the structure together with their operating and maintenance manuals. These also to include maintenance schedules

• drawings and schedules advising on the location and type of public utilities and services provided for the facility. This should include:

- emergency telephone numbers

- emergency 'shut down' procedures

- details of fire fighting systems

- details of alarm systems and how to test and operate them.

# 9 Bridge project

## 9.1 INTRODUCTION

This example describes the approach that might be adopted by the designer of a bridge to be used as part of an expansion scheme for an existing estate. The project is fictitious.

The design is progressed through four stages:

- preliminary
- concept
- scheme
- detailed.

During the preliminary and concept stages the project and main element issues are under consideration and decisions affect multiple work sections. Subsequent design stages examine the hazards on a work section basis. The development for this example is diagrammatically shown in Figure 14. Figure 15 contains the elements based on the CESSM3 work sections classification. (These two figures are included at the end of this section).

For the purposes of this example, the staged health and safety plans have been drawn up for incorporation into the relevant design reports prepared at the end of each design stage. The pre-tender stage health and safety plan has been prepared in accordance with Appendix 4 of the Approved Code of Practice.

To keep the example to a reasonable length, only certain aspects of the design have been addressed. It is not proposed that the solution is necessarily the optimum for the circumstances.

## 9.2 PROJECT INFORMATION

### 9.2.1 Location

The client currently owns a development on land adjacent to the main line railway. He has recently acquired some neighbouring land on the other side of the railway and beyond a river which runs alongside the railway. The general arrangement is shown in the key plan in Figure 12.

### 9.2.2 Client requirements

The client requires access to the newly acquired land. This entails crossing the main line railway and river. A 3.5m wide access is needed to carry the current range of vehicles and machinery and any vehicles he may purchase in the future. Separate walkways for pedestrians are not required. The client needs free access and does not wish to be restricted by level crossings over the railway.

### 9.2.3 Local environment

The two-track railway carries two diesel powered trains per hour in each direction, at high speed, throughout the day and one train per hour throughout the night. The river, a former industrial waterway, is now used for leisure purposes and is particularly busy in the summer months. The river is tidal and causes flooding of the surrounding land on average twice a year. It is probable that the silt in the river is contaminated with industrial waste products; hence disturbance of the silt will not be permitted.

The client's advisors have undertaken preliminary discussions with the railway and river authorities and he understands the considerable constraints that the requirement for possessions of both rail and river could exert during construction. In particular, a long lead time is required to book possessions of the railway because no possibility for diversion exists. This will have to coincide with other track maintenance work. Use of the river for access and major floating plant will not be allowed.

### 9.2.4 Site layout

The site layout, showing a possible solution using a bridge arrangement, is shown in Figure 12.

## 9.3 PRELIMINARY STUDY STAGE

### 9.3.1 Discussion of health and safety issues

*Identification of primary health and safety issues*

There are three main issues inherent to the site and neighbourhood:

- a tidal river, liable to flooding
- a two-track main line high speed railway
- a working development.

*Identification of the principal hazards in construction*

The principal hazards are thought to be:

- working on, over or near a variable level waterway
- working adjacent to and over operational railway lines.

*Review of possible design solutions for the crossing*

Studies revealed that no other location exists for an economic crossing of the railway and river which will avoid the need to deal with the hazards inherent to the location.

The client requires free access across the railway lines and river. This precludes the provision of an at-grade crossing of the railway lines and a river bridge. A tunnel structure, either by cut and cover method or thrust bore, was therefore compared with a bridge structure passing over both railway and river.

A brief study only was required to demonstrate that a tunnel would be far more expensive than a bridge, particularly in the light of difficult geotechnical conditions.

Health and safety considerations weighed heavily in favour of the bridge in the light of the hazards associated with tunnelling under an operational railway, coupled with the high water table and the risk of flooding in the area. The risks involved with constructing a bridge would be less than with a tunnel, although it is recognised that significant hazards remain.

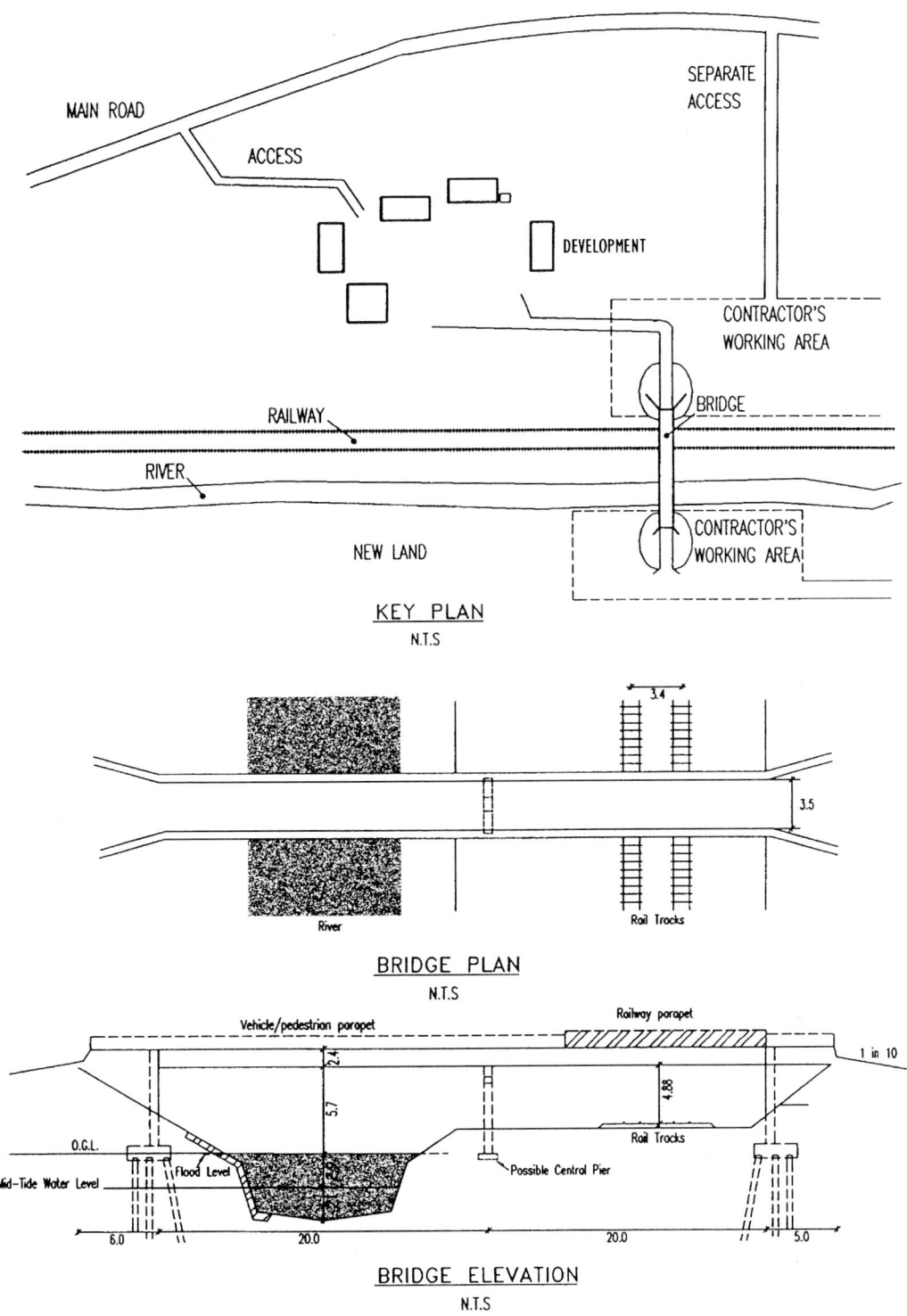

**Figure 12** *Key plan, bridge plan and bridge elevation*

It was agreed with the client at this early stage that a separate temporary access to the site would be necessary to avoid construction plant using the existing roads and to isolate the development from many of the hazards arising from the contractor's vehicle movements.

*Initial assessment of the level of competency required*

Is the work routinely safely carried out and are the hazards familiar to a competent design team and contractor?

At this stage it is assumed that the principal hazards are familiar to the designers. Contractors who tender for the work will undergo careful selection to ensure competency. Detailed method statements and safety plans will be part of the contractual requirements.

## 9.3.2    Preliminary stage health and safety plan

The health and safety issues will be recorded as follows in the Preliminary Stage health and safety plan which forms part of the Preliminary Stage Report.

### The site

It is proposed that construction of a dedicated separate access for construction purposes is included in the contract. The river cannot be used for access and this eliminates the hazard of building a temporary jetty on an unstable area adjacent to the river. However, it is proposed that temporary access across both the river and railway lines is provided for workers; this requirement cannot be avoided.

The Site Plan will need to show:

*   indication of known power lines, underground cables, pipework etc.
*   public rights of ways
*   accesses.

The other essential items of information required include railway authorities' restrictions; river authorities' restrictions; and Geotechnical Survey Report.

### The river

The tidal river over which the bridge is to be built is a former industrial waterway, now only used for leisure purposes. It is particularly busy in the summer months. The presence of the river means construction work and future maintenance will take place near and over water and this is a hazard. Early discussions with the river authorities are needed to incorporate their detailed requirements into subsequent design decisions.

The surrounding area is low-lying and liable to flooding in the winter months following heavy rain. The water table is generally within 1m of the flood plain surface. Flooding is a hazard to be taken into account in the design of the bridge, site layout and general logistics. Access to the site by the river and use of floating plant will not be allowed. This reduces the risk of disturbing contaminated silt from the previous industrial activity.

The high water table makes the stability of the areas adjacent to the river uncertain and this is a hazard for access to the area between the railway and river, and the riverside abutment.

### The railway

The railway over which the bridge is to be built is a two-track main line, carrying two diesel powered trains per hour in each direction throughout the day and one train per hour during the night. Construction work and future maintenance adjacent to this main line is a major hazard. Early discussions with the railway authorities are needed to incorporate their detailed requirements into subsequent design considerations, into the pre-tender stage health and safety plan, and hence into the contractor's works programme.

*Concept design stage*

The following design considerations are to be undertaken to minimise risks to health and safety:

- maximum use of pre-fabricated units for the bridge beams and deck in order to minimise in-situ work over the railway and river
- elimination of a central pier
- the design of the abutments, taking into account the ground conditions and the proximity of railway and river
- protection measures against trains
- protection measures against river vessel impacts
- avoid disturbance of river silts
- protection measures against flooding
- safe access for future maintenance and repair.

### 9.3.3 Designer's contribution to the health and safety file

The health and safety file will be opened and will contain the initial Preliminary Study Report, recommending the location of the crossing and the basis of the decision to build a bridge.

## 9.4 CONCEPT DESIGN STAGE

### 9.4.1 Discussion of health and safety issues

*Examination of bridge options and hazard elimination*

Outline schemes for different bridge arrangements using pre-fabricated beams with and without a central pier were examined, taking into account the following:

- access
- methods of construction
- sequences of construction
- programme
- costs
- health and safety
- risk assessments.

If the central pier can be eliminated and the bridge beams span from abutment to abutment using pre-fabricated beams, the overall health and safety risk on the project will be significantly reduced. This will also sit comfortably with the most likely preferred solution, taking into account cost and buildability.

The preferred solution is a single span bridge utilising I section steel beams. The deck will be formed from a series of simple pre-cast concrete units, stitched to the steel beams. Finally, an in-situ concrete slab will be placed over the pre-cast units to form continuity and a base for the water proofing and final surfacing. The general arrangement is shown in Figure 13.

This solution eliminates the central pier, but significant hazards remain. It is not possible to avoid some working at height over the railway and river during the placement of the beams and pre-cast deck units. However, design of the deck units will include an upstand as the base for the bridge parapets. This will allow provision of a temporary guard rail against falls during placement of the deck units and concreting of the in-situ slab, waterproofing and surfacing. Any need for temporary bracing of the steel beams during construction will be incorporated in the permanent structure.

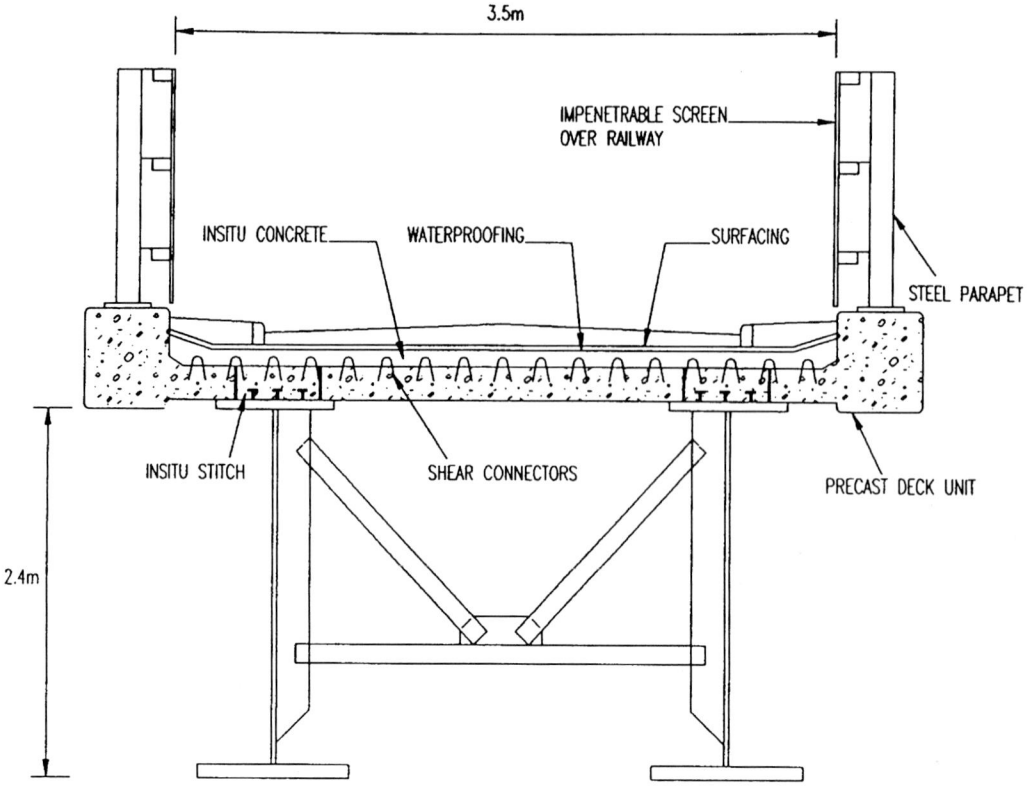

**Figure 13** *Rail/River Bridge - Deck Cross Section*

Methods of construction identified for the beam placing operation ranged from the single lift placement of the full length beam to the need for a temporary trestle support at a position between the railway and river. A bolted splice would then be undertaken in situ. Clearly, from a health and safety point of view, the single lift placement is preferable.

The design of the abutments requires piling to overcome the ground conditions. The piling on the railway side in particular will be designed to accommodate groups of piles that can be installed so that the operation of appropriate piling plant does not conflict with the safety requirements of the railway authorities. The methods will need to be discussed and approved by the railway operator. The piling on the river bank will be carried out with special safety measures in place to counter bank instability and flooding.

The type of piling wall will be addressed in the next design stage. Choice will not be constrained by the need to restrict noise from driving steel piles as the site is located away from residential areas.

The selection of steel beams for the bridge raises the question of the health and safety risks associated with periodic maintenance painting. The two principal issues are access and materials to be used. Frequency of planned maintenance will be set at 1 in 15 years - hence the rate of exposure to risk is limited.

It is proposed to eliminate the risks involved with maintenance of the bridge bearings by the design of an integrated beam and abutment.

### Identification of health and safety issues relating to the key areas

*Site*

- access and egress points
- working areas adjacent to river and railway
- temporary crossing of railway and river for workers
- storage areas for fuel and combustibles
- pollution of river
- welfare facilities.

*River works*

- piling adjacent to river
- excavation adjacent to river with high water levels
- protection against flooding
- concrete construction near water
- placement of bridge beams
- working on bridge over water
- future maintenance.

*Railway works*

- piling adjacent to railway
- excavation adjacent to railway
- protection of and against trains
- concrete construction near railway
- placement of bridge beams
- working on bridge over railway
- future maintenance.

### Identification of health and safety issues relating to:

*Construction methods for:*

- excavation support
- piling to abutments
- concreting abutments
- placing bridge beams
- bridge deck construction.

*Construction sequences and programme*

- sequence of abutment construction
- sequence of beam placing and deck construction
- programme and site congestion.

*Maintenance and repairs*

- repairs to expansion joints
- repairs to deck waterproofing
- access for painting steel beams
- repair to parapets.

*Assessment of the level of competency required*

Is the work routinely and safely carried out and are the hazards familiar to a competent design team and contractor?

It is assumed that the design remains familiar to the designer and contractor who will be invited to tender for the work. However, piling adjacent to the railway and river will require special precautions.

### 9.4.2 Concept design stage health and safety plan

The health and safety issues will be recorded in the Concept Design Stage health and safety plan which forms part of the Concept Design Report.

*The site*

The only site access and egress point is to be at the end of the temporary access road as it joins the site boundary fence. The working areas adjacent to the railway and river will need special precautions. Crossing of the railway and river for workers will need to be included in the site layout proposals. The storage areas for fuel and combustibles will need to have dedicated areas with allowance for flooding in order not to interfere with general site movements and to avoid the risk of river pollution. Likewise the welfare facilities will need special consideration.

The following hazardous operations have been identified for each area of works and need to be considered in the next design stage.

*River works*

- piling near river
- river bank protection works
- excavation with high water level
- construction of abutment and central pier near water
- placement of bridge beams
- placing of pre-cast deck units.

*Railway works*

- crane lifting operations adjacent to railway
- piling work adjacent to railway
- excavations and concrete construction adjacent to railway
- placement of bridge beams.

*Maintenance and repair*

- access to bridge beams for painting
- replacement of bridge surfacing
- replacement of expansion joints
- maintenance of parapets.

*Scheme Design Stage*

The following design considerations are to be undertaken to minimise risks to health and safety:

- examination of the possible beam placing methods
- examination of working on the flood plain with high water table and bank instability
- assessment of preferred type of piles for abutments

- design into the beams provision for pre-fabricated parapet units to provide a barrier to falls
- development of an outline construction programme that does not include the use of railway possessions for the construction of the abutment adjacent to the railway lines
- the provision for long periods between cycles of maintenance and repair to reduce the hazards of working near and over the railway and the river.

### 9.4.3 Designer's contribution to the health and safety file

The health and safety file is developed to include details of the design decisions reached in the Concept Design Stage.

## 9.5 SCHEME DESIGN STAGE

### 9.5.1 Discussion of health and safety issues

*Examination of design development and hazard elimination*

The major hazard of constructing the central pier has been eliminated. However, the safe method of beam installation needs to be addressed by the design team. The assumptions are to be recorded for consideration at the next design stage and are eventually passed to the contractor.

The location dictates that the bridge beams will have to be transported to the site in sections, most probably two, and jointed on site. It is thought that the preferred method of placing the beams will be by a single lift placement. This entails jointing the beams adjacent to one abutment and using a crane located either adjacent to one abutment or centrally between railway and river. Alternatively, the beam could be assembled in place with a temporary trestle located between the railway and river for the beam jointing operation. Whichever method is selected by the contractor, a beam joint will be necessary and details of this will be included in the design. Final details will be decided by the contractor in association with the beam fabricator. Hazards exist in both methods. These will be brought to the contractor's attention and he will be asked to respond in detailed method statements. Clearly, the interaction with the railway operations will need careful planning in co-ordination with the railway authorities.

The first consideration in carrying out the abutment piling is to the safety of the work in relation to the railway and river. The contractor will need to include provision of tensioned wire mesh screens alongside the rail track. Choice of piling system requires a comparison between the risks associated with bored piles, using bentonite, and driven steel tubes. It was considered that the use of bentonite was a risk to health, and might cause pollution of the river. Under the circumstances, it was decided to specify steel tube piles. The contractor will be asked to provide detailed method statements for carrying out the work adjacent to the railway and close to the river.

A programme has been developed that includes overnight railway possessions, but work adjacent to passing trains cannot be eliminated.

*Identification of work sections in relation to hazards that have not been eliminated*

Work sections affected by the hazards (Ref: CESMM3):

A     General items
G     Geotechnical

E     Earthworks
F/G   In-situ concrete
H     Pre-cast concrete
M    Structural steelwork
P/Q   Piles
R     Roads and paving
S     Rail track
V     Painting
W    Waterproofing

### *Health and safety hazards and risks arising from design parameters and assumptions on a work section basis*

To avoid repetition, the various hazardous operations in relation to the work sections are not given here but are listed in Section 9.5.2.

For this example, the hazardous operation of constructing the railway abutment and working adjacent to the railway requires specific risk assessment under each work section heading, i.e. E, F/G, P/Q.

### *Assessment of risks involved for each work section*

A qualitative assessment of the risks involved for work on piling at the railway abutment using steel tubular piles (Work Section P) has been carried out and is presented in Table 1 (Reference: *Designing for Health and Safety in Construction*, HSE). Such an assessment would be carried out for all work sections. The results of the risk assessment are then used in the application of the principles of protection (see Table 2).

### *Assessment of the level of competency required*

In conjunction with the planning supervisor, assess the level of competency required. Are the work sections routinely safely carried out by a competent contractor? This will enable the planning supervisor to advise the client on the competency of contractors invited to tender.

## 9.5.2    Scheme design stage health and safety plan

### *Remaining hazards*

It has not been possible to eliminate all the hazards associated with the following:

- working over and adjacent to railway
- working over, on or near river
- working on flood plain for abutment
- maintenance and repair.

Efforts will be made to reduce and control the above hazards, based on the results of the work section risk assessments.

The following hazardous operations and issues have been identified, but not eliminated, at this stage and need to be considered in the next design stage on a work section basis. Assessments have been carried out to ascertain the risks involved (see Table 1) and these indicate that the effects of the hazards need to be reduced for the following work sections (see Figure 15).

**Table 1** Risk Assessment

| Hazards | Persons at risk | | | Severity of harm | | | Likelihood of harm | | | Risk acceptable Y/N |
|---|---|---|---|---|---|---|---|---|---|---|
| | Employ | Public | Vist. | H | M | L | H | M | L | |
| 1. Dust | ✓ | - | - | - | - | ✓ | - | - | ✓ | Y |
| 2. Noise/Vib | ✓ | - | - | - | ✓ | - | ✓ | - | - | N |
| 3. Handling | ✓ | - | - | - | ✓ | - | ✓ | - | - | N |
| 4. Plant | ✓ | - | - | ✓ | - | - | ✓ | - | - | N |
| 5. Objects | ✓ | - | - | ✓ | - | - | ✓ | - | - | N |
| 6. Falls | ✓ | ✓ | ✓ | ✓ | - | - | ✓ | - | - | N |
| 7. Tripping | ✓ | ✓ | ✓ | - | - | ✓ | ✓ | - | - | Y |
| 8. Substances | ✓ | - | - | - | - | ✓ | - | - | ✓ | Y |
| 9. Railway | - | ✓ | - | ✓ | - | - | ✓ | - | - | N |

**Table 2** Application of principles of protection

| Hazards | Avoid | Combat at source | Communal | Personal |
|---|---|---|---|---|
| 1. Dust | Risk OK | - | - | - |
| 2. Noise/Vib | Not possible | Yes | Specify hammer enclosure | Ear muffles |
| 3. Handling | Not possible | Yes | Provide attachment points | Self release shackles |
| 4. Plant | Not possible | Yes | Provide working space | Planning |
| 5. Objects | Not possible | Yes | Provide working space | Planning |
| 6. Falls | Not possible | Yes | Provide walkways | Harnesses, manlocks etc |
| 7. Tripping | Risk OK | - | - | - |
| 8. Substances | Risk OK | - | - | - |
| 9. Railway | Not possible | Yes | Screens | Procedures |

## A General items - temporary works

- general working near river and railway
- provision of temporary access across river and railway.

## E Earthworks

- stability of excavations with high water table
- flooding levels
- plant access for piling and excavation
- excavation support.

## F/G In-situ concrete

- concreting walls adjacent to river (includes formwork and rebar)
- concreting wall adjacent to railway (includes formwork and rebar)
- concreting abutment on the flood plain.

## M Structural Steelwork

- transport of beams to site
- beam placing.

## P/Q Piling

- installation adjacent to railway
- installation adjacent to river bank on flood plain.

### The site

The following issues and the associated hazards need to be considered in the next stage:

- location of site accommodation to allow for flooding
- site boundary fencing for security
- location of crossing points for workers over the railway and river.

### Maintenance and repair

The following hazardous operations have been previously identified and need to be considered further in the next design stage:

- painting of bridge beams
- replacement of bridge surfacing
- replacement of expansion joints
- repairs to parapets.

### Construction methods, sequences and programme

- construction methods assumed for design purposes
- construction sequences and programme assumed for design purposes.

### Detailed design stage

The following design considerations are to be undertaken:

- the identified hazards for each work section that have not been eliminated are reviewed against published guidance information in order to reduce their effect and achieve control during the construction work, future maintenance and repair.

### 9.5.3 Designer's contributions to the health and safety file

The file is developed to incorporate details of the design decisions finalised during the scheme design stage. Details of materials and initial considerations of the strategy for maintenance, repair and demolition are to be included.

## 9.6. DETAILED DESIGN STAGE

### 9.6.1 Discussion of health and safety issues

*Elimination of hazards*

At the detailed design stage the major design options have been closed off because the design must be frozen at the end of scheme design. Hence, the main objective regarding health and safety is to reduce the effects of known hazards and achieve control of these during the construction work.

*Review design details for each work section*

The reduction and control of hazards and risks on a work section basis needs to be based on experience of working methods and sequences. In particular, buildability assessments are essential. For this example, assessments would be carried out for each work section based on those carried out at the scheme design stage (see Section 9.5.1).

To take one example - F/G In-situ concrete:

* recognised hazards, e.g. falling from height off scaffold
* formwork operations adjacent to railway
* sufficient working space for formwork props?, use of cross ties to avoid props?
* reinforcement arrangements, length of bars restricted?
* access for truck mixer?, use of pumping
* working at height on deck slab over railway and river.

*Construction method, sequences and programme*

Review:

* construction methods, and
* construction sequences and programme

assumed for design purposes.

*Identify maintenance and repair strategy for each work section*

* frequency of maintenance inspections
* maintenance access
* materials for:
  - waterproofing
  - surfacing
  - painting.

### 9.6.2 Detailed design stage health and safety plan

The details of the designer's contributions are outlined in the next section as his inputs to the pre-tender stage health and safety plan.

## 9.7 THE STRUCTURAL ENGINEER'S CONTRIBUTION TO THE PRE-TENDER STAGE HEATH AND SAFETY PLAN*

### 1. General

*All prospective main contractors tendering for this contract will receive this health and safety plan. The purpose is to highlight the main health and safety issues in connection with the construction work on the project and to form a basis for tenderers to explain their proposals for managing the problems.*

*The principal contractor will develop this health and safety plan as part of his duties, in particular taking reasonable steps to ensure co-operation between all contractors to achieve compliance with the rules and recommendations of the plan.*

### 2. Nature of project

Name of Client: *A Developer Ltd*

Location: *A rural location adjacent to an area of previous medium sized industrial activity.*

The construction
work: *The work entails the construction of an access bridge crossing a main railway and tidal river. The form of construction is steel beams with pre-cast concrete deck units. The abutments are piled and built in situ.*

Timescale for completion
of construction work: *The proposed timescale for the work is six months.*

### 3. The existing environment

*The client currently owns land adjacent to a main line railway. He has recently acquired some neighbouring land on the other side of the railway and beyond a river which runs alongside the railway. The client requires free access for vehicles to his newly acquired land. This entails crossing the main line railway and river by bridge.*

*The two-track railway carries two diesel powered trains per hour in each direction at high speed throughout the day and one train per hour throughout the night. The river is a former industrial waterway, now used for leisure purposes and is particularly busy in the summer months. The river is tidal and liable to cause flooding in the surrounding land on average twice a year. It is probable that the silt in the river is contaminated with industrial products and hence disturbance of the silt is not permitted.*

### 4. Existing drawings

*Existing topographical and geotechnical surveys and reports are available as follows:*

---

* In this example plan, the case study designer's inputs to the plan are shown in bold face and the inputs of all others are shown in italics.

- *Topographical maps, Nos A, B and C*
- *Geotechnical Survey Report, reference X, Y and Z.*

## 5. The design

Hazards and work sequences have been identified during the design which cannot be avoided and which will be a risk to the health and safety of construction workers. These are divided into two categories:

(a) where standard known solutions apply that will minimise and control risks
(b) where standard known solutions do not apply and special provisions are required.

It should be noted that standard known solutions are not free from risk and appropriate measures must be taken by contractors to minimise and/or control these risks.

The specific hazards and assessed risks are outlined below for each work section affected and designated category (a) or (b) (as defined above). The list does not address the common-place site hazards which must be controlled by the application of normal good site management practices.

**Work Section**

**A  General Items**

- temporary works for construction and site facilities near or over the river and railway (b).

**E  Earthworks**

- proximity of railway and river (b)
- high water table (b)
- flooding levels (b)
- access for plant (a)
- excavation support (a).

**F/G  In-situ concrete**

- construction of abutment adjacent to the railway (b)
- construction of abutment adjacent to the river (b).

**H  Pre-cast concrete**

- placing deck units on steel beams (b)
- in-situ stitch to steel beams (b).

**M  Structural steelwork**

- transport and assembly of bridge beams (a)
- beam placing by crane (b).

**P/Q  Piling**

- installation adjacent to railway (b)
- installation adjacent to river bank on flood plain (b).

**V  Painting**

- in-situ touch-up painting of bridge beam (a).

**W Waterproofing**

- in-situ application of bitumastic materials on bridge deck (a).

The principles of the structural design for the bridge are those traditionally adopted for Department of Transport structures. Particular attention was paid to the design of the abutments piling located in the flood plain of the river and adjacent to the railway. The bridge beams have been designed as simply supported and the possible methods installation for the beams was taken into account in the design. A joint has been detailed which will facilitate the assembly of the beam on site, either in readiness for a single lift or in place utilising a temporary trestle at about mid-span between railway and river.

The specific problems where contractors are required to explain their proposals for health and safety management during the construction stage are outlined below:

- layout of site facilities and temporary accesses
- procedures for safety for the river and railway
- procedures for safety in case of flooding
- protection against river vessel and train impacts
- protection measures for working adjacent and over railway
- protection measures for working near and over river
- methods of working in flood plain for: piling, excavation and in-situ concrete work
- methods of working adjacent to railway for: piling, excavation and in-situ concrete work
- methods and procedures for bridge beams:
    - fabrication
    - transport to site
    - jointing at site
    - placement over railway and river
- methods and procedures for bridge deck:
    - pre-cast concrete units, manufacture and placing
    - in-situ concrete
    - waterproofing
    - surfacing
    - parapets.

## 6.      Construction materials

The following health hazards from materials have been identified which cannot be avoided and which will be a risk to the health of construction workers:

- waterproofing - bituminous mastic between layers
- bridge beams - protection paint work.

## 7.      Site wide elements

The following hazards have been identified which cannot be avoided and which will be a risk to the safety of construction workers:

- site access and egress points
- location of site accommodation to avoid flooding
- lay down areas and storage to avoid flooding
- temporary access across river and railway
- location of fuel and combustibles.

## 8.      Overlap with client's undertaking

*Due consideration is to be given to the developer's ongoing operations. Access through his existing farm building has been eliminated by the designation of a separate access for the sole use of the contractor.*

## 9.       Site Rules

Rules have been devised under the following headings to control the risks arising from the identified hazards:

*   *site permits to be obtained by all persons entering site*
*   *emergency procedures for flash flooding*
*   *site training*
*   *permanent attendance of Railtrack personnel*
*   *railway permits from Railtrack*
*   *wearing of life-jackets when working above water*
*   *screen alongside railway*
*   *warning signs and temporary dolphins on river*
*   *safety boat attendance on river.*

## 10.      Continuing liaison

*Procedures for consideration and acceptance of the health and safety implications of design elements by the principal contractor and other contractors' packages are as follows:*

*   *submit details of the health and safety issues to the planning supervisor, including results of appropriate risk assessments*

*   *in particular, implications arising from the design of temporary works will be required well in advance of the execution of the work to allow full consideration.*

*Procedures for dealing with unforeseen eventualities during project execution which result in substantial design changes and which might affect resources are as follows:*

*   *as soon as an unforeseen eventuality arises, the planning supervisor is to be informed by the principal contractor*

*   *the health and safety issues arising are to be submitted to the planning supervisor as soon as possible after the event*

*   *details of the re-design and the health and safety implications are to be submitted for consideration and acceptance in due time before execution to the planning supervisor via the principal contractor.*

## 9.8   THE HEALTH AND SAFETY FILE

The inputs to the health and safety file are brought together by the planning supervisor into a consolidated document that marks a distinct stage of the development at the end of detailed design.

It will be consistent with the health and safety plan and describe the health and safety information available at the end of detailed design.  This will include:

*   Site survey
*   Design criteria
*   Materials to be incorporated into the structure
*   Outline methods of construction assumed for design purposes
*   Construction sequences and programme assumed for design purposes
*   Maintenance, repair and demolition strategy.

The file will be added to during the construction stage.

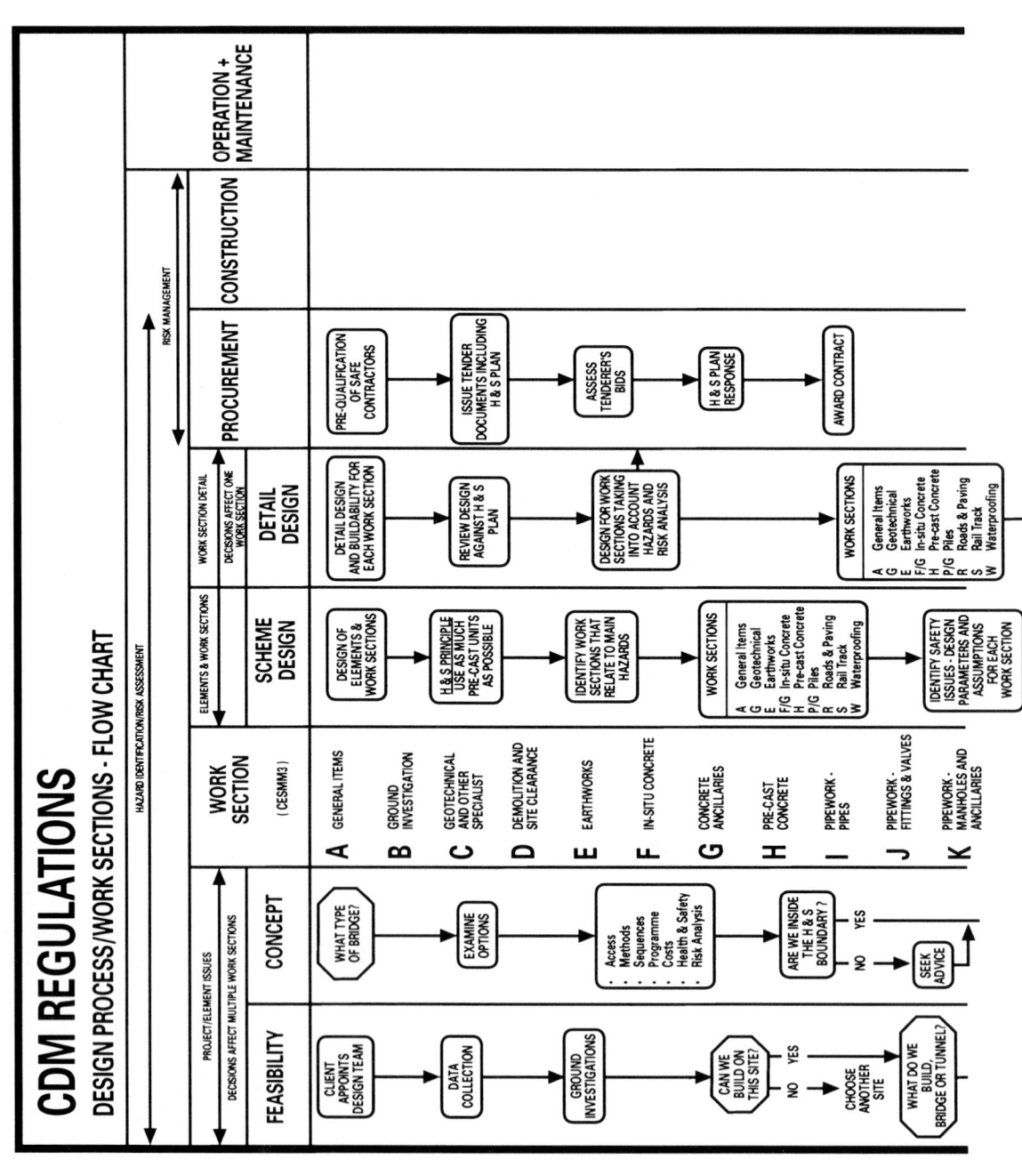

**Figure 14** *Design Process/Work Section Flow Chart*

CIRIA Report 145

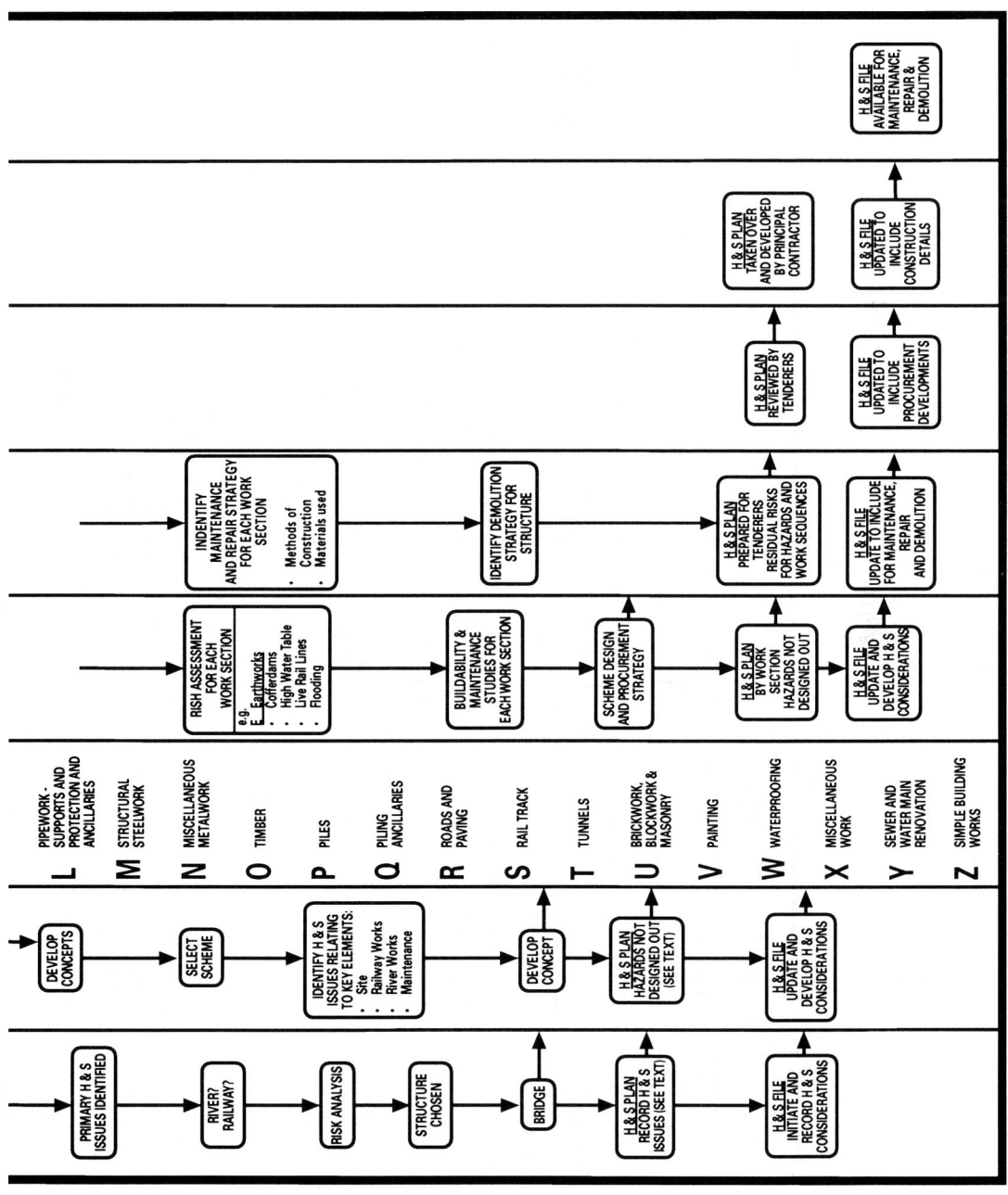

**Figure 15** *Elements and Work Sections*

CDM - Designers' Handbooks

Grouping the Civil Engineering Work Sections in Elements

**Basis - Civil Engineering: CESMM3 Work Classification (see Figure 14)**

**Class**

| | | |
|---|---|---|
| 1. | **General Items/Preliminaries** | A |
| 2. | **Demolition and site clearance** | D |
| 3. | **Groundworks (incl. piling)** | B, C, E, P, Q |
| 4. | **Concrete Structures** | F, G, H |
| 5. | **Steelwork Structures** | M, N |
| 6. | **Other Structures** | O |
| 7. | **Surfacing** | R |

8. **Particular Facilities**
   - Railways (S) Tunnels (T)                    S, T
   - Highways                                    R
   - Sewers                                      Y
   - Marine works                                -
   - Small buildings                             Z
   - Pipework                                    I, J, K, L

| | | |
|---|---|---|
| 9. | **Mechanical, Electrical, HVAC** | - |
| 10. | **Finishes** | V, W, X |
| 11. | **Maintenance** | - |

Sections refer to CESMM3.

# 10 Retaining wall project

## 10.1 INTRODUCTION

This example describes the approach adopted by the designer of a retaining wall built as part of an urban road scheme. It is based on a real situation although some aspects have been modified for the sake of clarity and not all technical considerations have been described.

The design is progressed through three stages:

* concept
* outline
* detailed.

## 10.2 PROJECT INFORMATION

### 10.2.1 Background

The scheme is an urban highway improvement within a proposed development area. The client, the Development Corporation, has identified the area for social, environmental and industrial regeneration. The proposed road link forms a major regional and local transport artery of commercial and residential significance. Completion of this project is a necessary prerequisite of regeneration in the area.

### 10.2.2 Scheme requirements and location

The proposed scheme, as shown in Figure 16, requires construction of a dual two-lane carriageway. Connections with existing roundabouts tie the scheme into the present highway network. The chosen option has been carefully developed through a comprehensive and detailed public consultation and inquiry procedure.

The site, which the client has already acquired, is adjacent to residential and commercial properties. Site clearance has already been undertaken with all properties demolished to existing ground level. There is no existing road on the proposed highway route.

### 10.2.3 Environmental concerns

The overall scheme objectives included a desire to mitigate the effects of severance, noise, visual intrusion and land take. This meant the carriageway surface of a certain length of the road would have to be constructed eight metres below existing ground level. Appropriate forms of retaining structure were, therefore, a necessary requirement.

Part of the site was previously used for industrial purposes, with contaminated soil present on a confined area.

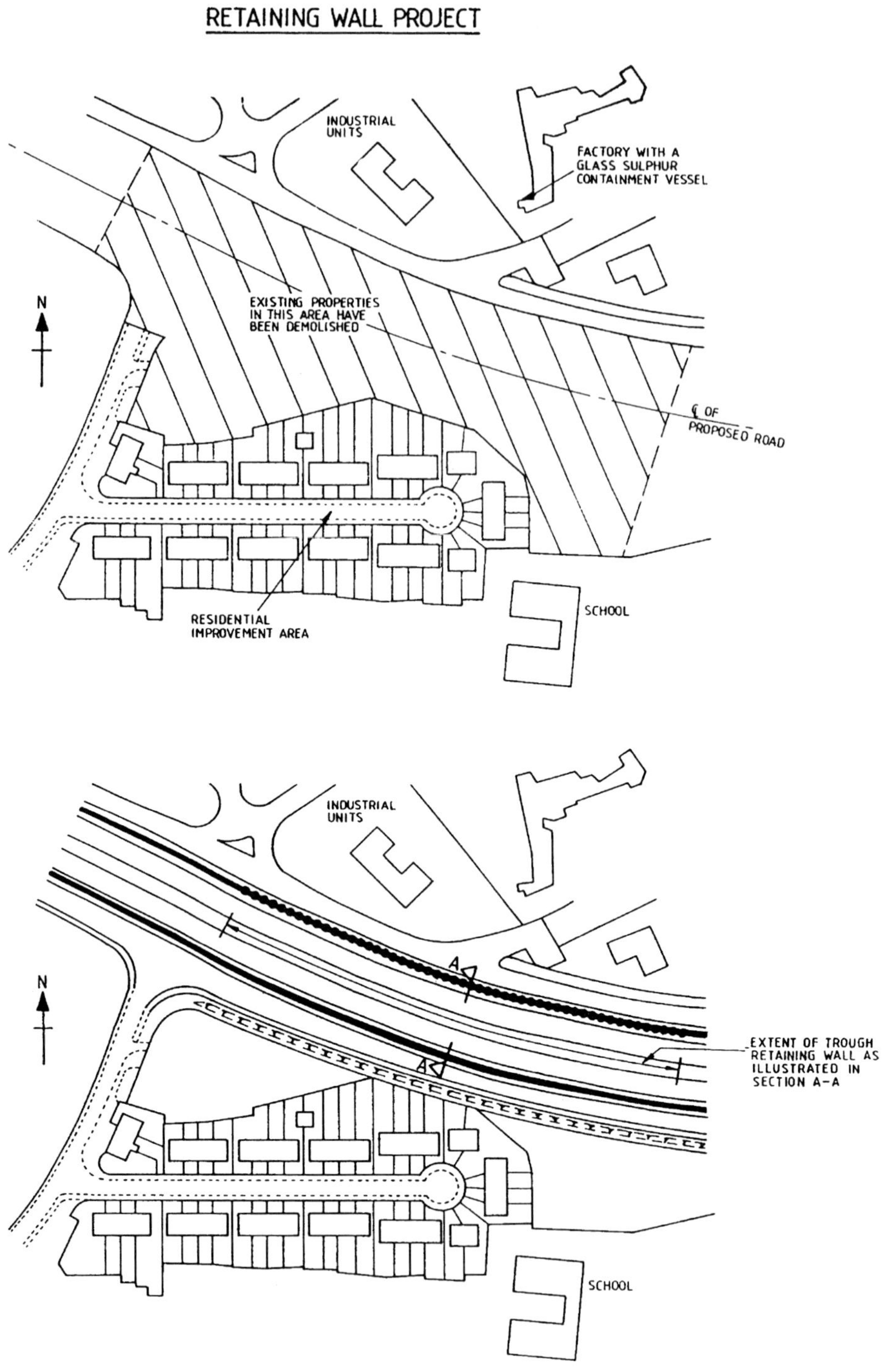

**Figure 16** *Existing site and proposed scheme plan*

## 10.2.4   Retaining wall

The retaining wall project developed consists of a reinforced concrete trough section with walls of cantilever or contiguous pile construction (see Figure 17). The trough will be approximately eight metres deep. A reinforced concrete slab forms the trough floor which acts as a structural prop to the piles and is an integral part of the road pavement construction.

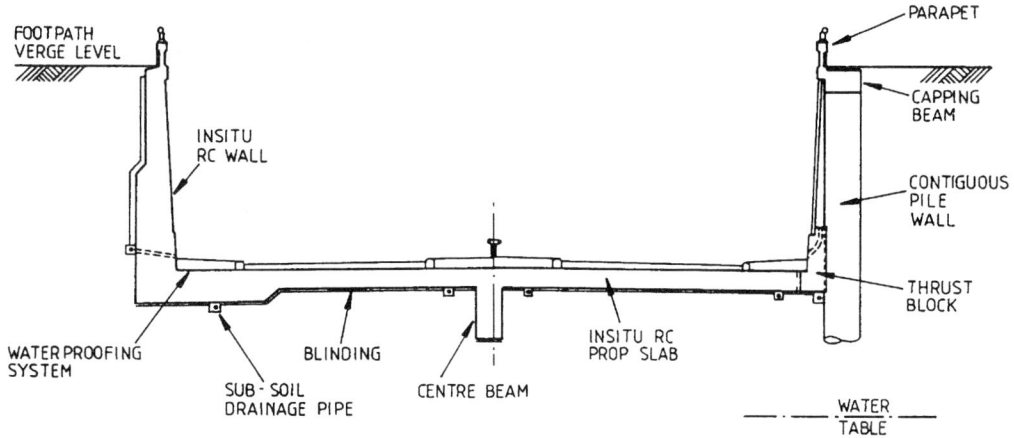

**Figure 17** *Section A-A*

## 10.3 CONCEPT DESIGN STAGE

### 10.3.1 Discussion of health and safety issues

The preliminary site investigation, soil survey and desk study identify the criteria to be considered when assessing the feasibility of the proposals. The following health and safety issues are identified at the concept design stage.

### *Adjacent building occupiers*

The site is adjacent to both residential and industrial areas. Consider effects of:

- noise
- vibration
- dust

on occupiers of adjacent buildings, which are of the following categories:

- domestic residential buildings
- commercial/industrial properties
- public buildings - schools, hospitals, old peoples' homes.

The following issues appear relevant:

- The nearest domestic residential properties are situated about 10m from the site. Limiting effects of constructional noise, vibration and dust is therefore a material consideration throughout the design.

- A small industrial estate is identified adjacent to the site. One factory unit has a glass sulphur containment vessel which is sensitive to vibration. Consideration should be given to interaction with effects of construction.

- No public building is directly adjacent to the site although an infant and junior school are within the general locality. Security of any proposed construction site is a necessary consideration, particularly where children are concerned.

- Effects of gaseous emissions and fire on adjacent buildings and their occupiers.

### *Stability of buildings and structures*

Several factors affecting the structural stability of existing buildings in close proximity to the works have been identified and will require detailed consideration during the design. These include:

- Some older residential properties are constructed on a gravel type material. Foundations of these buildings are expected to be corbeled brickwork or stone. Excessive vibration close to these properties could cause consolidation of the gravel and the subsequent loss of foundations to buildings.

- Direct loss of foundations into excavations formed alongside buildings.

- Variations in the water table profile during and subsequent to construction may cause alterations in the founding soil characteristics. Detailed soil and groundwater investigations have determined a water table at a level just below foundation level which will need consideration during the design process.

- Disused mine workings have been identified in the area. They are sufficiently remote to be unaffected by construction although excessive ground vibration should be considered with regard to potential localised collapse.

### *General public*

The works will require construction adjacent to existing public roads. This will mean that:

- access for workers' and emergency vehicles will need to be maintained for two factory units

- closure of a public highway which runs alongside the works will not be permitted during any phase of construction. Therefore options for diversion will need to be considered

- conflict of pedestrian and vehicular rights of way with any proposed construction is identified as a possible hazard. Consideration of vehicle and pedestrian barriers required.

### *Statutory undertakers' services*

Various statutory undertakers' services have been identified within and adjacent to the site:

- gas
- electric
- telecommunications
- water
- street lighting.

The effect of proposals on each utility's existing apparatus and any required future provision will need to be considered.

The locations of existing fire hydrants, which are to be maintained, must be kept unobstructed and access free.

The effects of construction upon the existing lighting provision will need to be considered. Lighting must be maintained for road signs, pedestrian routes and carriageways.

### Contaminated land

Part of the site is derelict industrial land. Detailed soil and groundwater analyses for contamination identified:

- methane gas
- water soluble contaminates
- ground contaminates.

### Previous occupancy

There are no details or drawings available of hidden obstructions or foundations remaining on the site from its previous occupancy.

## 10.3.2   Designer's contributions to the health and safety plan and file

'F' in the right-hand margin denotes an item which should be incorporated in the project file and 'P' an item to be included in the plan.

The health and safety issues raised during the concept design stage which will be introduced by the designer into the plan and file include:

- domestic residential properties are close to the site. The effects of:

    - noise
    - vibration
    - dust

    will need to be limited                                                                                          P

- a vibration sensitive sulphur glass containment vessel is housed within an adjacent factory unit, and vibration from construction must be monitored and limited                                        P

- security to prevent or deter unauthorised entry onto the site from adjacent housing areas and nearby schools                                                                                       P

- gravel materials beneath some of the residential properties may undergo consolidation if subjected to vibration. Certain constructional techniques, such as pile driving, may cause loss of founding to these properties                                                                      P

- collapse of disused mine workings could be caused by excessive ground vibration              P/F

- vehicular and public rights of way are present within the site. Conflicts between construction and these rights of way need to be identified. Adjacent road diversions will need to be considered instead of closures. Vehicle and pedestrian barriers required                            P

- statutory undertakers' apparatus is present on or adjacent to the site                        P/F

    - gas
    - electric
    - telecommunications
    - water
    - street lighting
    - fire hydrants.

There may be conflict between construction and statutory undertakers' apparatus. See drawings.

- soil and groundwater analyses reveal the presence of:

    - methane gas
    - water soluble contaminates
    - ground contaminates.                                                     P/F

- the groundwater table throughout the site is just below structure foundation level     P/F

- there are no details or drawings available of hidden obstructions or foundations remaining
  on the site from its previous occupancy                                      P

- location of existing and proposed fire hydrants.  Existing locations, which are to be
  maintained, must be kept unobstructed and access free.  Responsible authorities and
  emergency services will be informed of their location.                       P/F


## 10.4  OUTLINE DESIGN STAGE

### 10.4.1  Discussion of health and safety issues

The health and safety issues identified at the concept design stage are taken as the basis of further
consideration when evaluating specific options for the outline design stage.

These issues include:

1.  Excessive noise and vibration levels which can arise from certain plant and constructional
    operations.

    Driving piles can cause unnecessary noise and vibration.  This activity may affect:

- integrity of a glass sulphur containment vessel
- consolidation of gravels beneath property foundations
- integrity of disused mine workings.

2.  The soil investigation identified:

- poor ground conditions and predicted difficulty in constructing open excavations in restricted
  areas.  Temporary works would be necessary

- a low acceptable ground bearing pressure.  Stability calculations to achieve factors of safety
  for sliding, overturning and rotation will need to be developed in detailed design.

3.  The possible seepage of bentonite type materials into mine workings, ducts and services.

4.  In the assessed soil conditions, ground anchors would have to extend beyond the general site
    boundary.  Heave and ground movement could be caused with detrimental effects on building
    stability.

5.  The congested site with restricted access and working space will require careful planning and
    organisation and, therefore, some site plant or operations may be precluded through lack of
    space.

6.  Liaison with statutory undertakers has identified:

- electricity
    - overhead wires requiring diversion

- underground cable adjacent to work but not directly affected
- substation with switch gear requiring protection from dust and vibration

- gas
  - main on site but unaffected by work

- water
  - diversion required

- telecommunications
  - diversion required

- street lighting
  - additional provision required.

7. Maintenance difficulties have been identified with certain structural elements which may have associated health and safety issues:

- ground anchors
- steel sheet piles.

Access for repair and maintenance is:

- alongside live carriageway, or
- elevated, or
- restricted or obstructed

and this will require specific design considerations to minimise the hazards implicit in each case.

8. Temporary works requiring particular consideration include:

- support during excavation
- elevated access
- formwork and shuttering.

The above issues associated with health and safety have been considered during examination of the following constructional options for the retaining wall:

- conventional reinforced concrete cantilever - area of open excavation required to accommodate base which includes both a toe and heel. Temporary works can be utilised to limit excavation

- contiguous or secant pile - limited area required for construction without requiring temporary works

- diaphragm wall - requires bentonite for construction

- steel-sheet piling - noise and vibration associated with installations

- reinforced earth - ground heave and areas required for construction

- mass concrete - area of open excavation required for construction.

It was concluded that the most appropriate form of construction would be a reinforced concrete trough section with in-situ walls of cantilever construction on one side and contiguous piles on the other. The trough floor slab acts as a structural prop to the piles and is an integral part of the road pavement construction. This structural form will be progressed through to detailed design.

### 10.4.2 Designer's contributions to the health and safety plan and file

The health and safety issues raised during the outline design stage which will be introduced by the designer into the plan and file include:

#### *Utilities*

- gas - main on site but unaffected by work                                                 P

- water - diversion required                                                                 P

- British Telecom - diversion required                                                       P

- electricity
    - overhead wires require diversion
    - underground cable on site but unaffected by work
    - substations with switch gear requiring protection from dust and vibration.             P

- street lighting - additional provision required.                                           P

Refer to drawings.

#### *Pile wall*

The reinforced concrete road pavement forms a structural prop to the contiguous pile wall; therefore, sequencing of construction is necessary. Removal of significant lengths of the road construction at a later date for maintenance etc. would cause structural instability to these walls.                                                                           F

#### *Soils investigation*

The soils investigation identified:

- poor ground conditions and predicted difficulty in constructing open excavations in restricted areas                                                                           P/F

- a low acceptable ground bearing pressure                                                   P

- excessive noise and vibration from plant and constructional operations                     P/F

- the possible seepage of bentonite type materials into mine workings, ducts and services.   P/F

## 10.5  DETAILED DESIGN STAGE

### 10.5.1  Discussion of health and safety issues

The consideration of health and safety issues brought forward from the previous stages is further developed in the detailed design. These issues include:

1. Contaminated land forming part of the site has been investigated further and found to be confined to a specific area.

The issues arising are:

- direct health risk to workers on site
- adjacent public neighbours affected by contaminated dust
- failure of structural elements due to contact with aggressive environment.

Contamination is to be dealt with under a separate advance contract prior to progress of construction work. Removal, transportation and disposal of contaminated ground is to be undertaken in a controlled manner during this advance contract.

2. Methane, identified in the locality, can be carried by local groundwater. Temporary ground excavations, permanent drainage runs, manholes or interceptors may contain methane gas. Vented manhole and interceptor covers are provided for surface water drainage.

3. Discussions with the Local Authority and Environmental Health Services Department have identified suitable access routes to the site.

4. Dust will be a problem for both site operatives and local residents. Consideration given to implementation of:

- site sprinkler system to suppress generation
- effective wheel washer to contain spread onto adjacent roads.

5. The surface finish to concrete walls will not be scabbled due to the increased generation of dust. An as-struck or cladding finish will be specified.

6. Various alternative pedestrian/vehicle parapets are examined, taking into account:

- safe access for maintenance
- enhanced pedestrian restraint due to location, i.e. schools and residential areas
- type of materials for long-term maintenance.

The above considerations resulted in a reinforced concrete wall with an additional steel rail.

7. A number of situations could give rise to a pollution risk to watercourses and groundwater. These will be minimised by one or more of the following measures:

- pollution of watercourses by surface water run-off from the road - this will be mitigated by the provision of interceptors

- contamination of watercourses from run-off during the earthwork operations - the contractor will provide temporary containment measures

- accidental spillages of petrol/oil - this will be mitigated by installation of interceptors in the drainage system.

Responsible authorities and emergency services will be informed of the location of the various interceptors to enable cleaning procedures to be carried out expeditiously after accidents, if necessary.

8. The importance of the following structural elements related to collapse during construction and maintenance has been identified:

- Pile capping beam    -    ties the top of all discrete piles together
- Centre beam          -    provides structural rigidity and stability
- Road pavement        -    acts as prop to the piles
- Thrust block         -    transfers prop force into piles.

9. The following construction sequence is thought feasible:

(i) Construct piles for contiguous pile wall.

(ii) Construct capping beams on piles.

(iii) Excavate for and construct the south half of trough structure remote from piles including centre beam. This in-situ RC wall opposite the piles may be backfilled to 1m above base slab at this stage. An element of original ground material as detailed on the drawings should remain undisturbed in front of the contiguous piles during this whole operation.

(iv) Excavate road side of contiguous piles subject to the following:

- excavate 1m below ground level and install temporary steel props and walings to top of wall

- excavate to 2m above final road level

- install second temporary steel props and walings at 3m above final road level

- complete excavation for trough slab.

(v) Construct thrust block and prop slab.

(vi) On completion of the prop slab, the south wall opposite to the piles should be backfilled to a minimum of 3m below finished ground level behind the wall.

A detailed construction statement and method sequence, including calculations and drawings, will be required from the contractor. The designer will specify maximum movements that can be tolerated.

Construction of reinforced concrete elements has been carefully considered for aspects of buildability. The reinforcement is scheduled to provide lengths of manageable size for the situations required and to allow construction joints for structural lifts where appropriate.

10. The use of solvent-based paint has been limited within the design. Parapets are of reinforced concrete and only a top steel feature rail requires painting. An aluminium rail was not suitable, although maintenance requirements were a consideration. Water-based protective paint systems were not thought appropriate due to their reduced durability and increased maintenance requirements. A solvent-based paint system has, therefore, been specified for the top steel feature rail.

11. All road carriageway drainage and services have been located above the structural slab forming the trough invert. This eliminates the requirement for excavation through the slab for maintenance purposes. The following design features are highlighted:

- carriageway drainage is integral within the kerb and verge

- interceptors are located in the drainage system off the trough structure

- drainage to the retaining wall discharges at the front face just above verge level. Water is then taken into a channel grating at the back of the verge. Connections are made from this drain into the main carriageway drain

- provision for statutory undertakers' apparatus is made within the verge.

12. Subsoil drainage incorporates vented manholes for inspection and maintenance. The drain construction includes porous flexible jointed pipes with porous concrete surround.

## 10.5.2  Designer's contribution to the health and safety plan and file

The health and safety issues raised during the detailed design stage which will be introduced by the designer into the plan and file include:

- Methane, identified locally, can be carried in groundwater. Temporary ground excavations, permanent drainage runs, manholes or interceptors may contain methane gas. Vented manhole and interceptor covers are provided for surface water drainage.      P/F

- Access routes to the site have been identified on drawings.      P

- Noise will be a problem for both site operatives and local residents, and the contractor should observe the Noise at Work Regulations.      P

- Dust will be a problem for both site operatives and local residents. Consideration given to implementation of controlling measures.      P

- Pollution of watercourses by surface water run-off from the road will be mitigated by the provision of drainage interceptors before discharge into the main storm water system. Responsible authorities and emergency services to be informed of interceptor locations.      F

- Contamination of watercourses from run-off during earthwork operations is identified as an issue for the contractor. They will need to supply a detailed construction statement and method sequence, including calculations.      P

- A possible sequence has been identified for trough construction which highlights the importance of various structural elements.      P/F

- The use of solvent-based paint has been limited within the design. Parapets are of reinforced concrete and only a top steel feature rail requires painting.      P/F

- All road carriageway drainage and services have been located above the structural slab forming the trough invert. This eliminates the requirement for excavation through the slab for maintenance purposes.      F

- Provision for statutory undertakers' apparatus has been made within the verge.      F

- Subsoil drainage incorporates vented manholes for inspection and maintenance.      F

## 10.6  THE CIVIL ENGINEER'S CONTRIBUTION TO THE PRE-TENDER STAGE HEALTH AND SAFETY PLAN*

### 1.      Nature of project

Name of client:              *A Development Corporation*

Location:                    *An urban location within a proposed development area. Residential and industrial development predominates with interspersed areas of derelict land of unknown previous usage.*

The construction work:       *Work entails construction of a dual two-lane carriageway. Connections with existing roundabouts tie the scheme into the present highway network.*

**A major part of the highway is contained within a reinforced concrete trough section sunk below existing ground level. The retaining walls to the trough are of cantilever wall and propped contiguous pile construction.**

Timescale for completion
of construction:             *A 16 month contract period is allowed for completion of the construction work.*

### 2.      The existing environment

*The client has previously carried out extensive public consultation on this proposed project. The public are fully informed of the scheme objectives, their requirements and the way in which they will be achieved. A public inquiry was held which resulted in final development of the present scheme. Use of retaining walls to reduce land take and the lowering of the road below existing ground level in order to reduce visual intrusion and noise were important features in that consideration.*

*All necessary land has been purchased by the client to allow construction of the scheme. Accommodation work for all residential and commercial properties along the route has been completed in advance of the proposed main contract. This work included:*

* *construction of fences, walls and access gates to residential and commercial properties*
* *provision of double glazing to some residential properties as part of compensation negotiations.*

*The client has started to carry out environmental enhancing measures for certain residential roads in the locality. These works include:*

* *road surface improvements and paving*
* *pedestrianisation*
* *improved street furniture*
* *vehicle carriageway width restrictions*
* *vehicle speed ramps*
* *residents' parking provision in association with general parking restrictions.*

---

\* In this example plan, the case study designer's inputs to the plan are shown in bold face, while the inputs of others are shown in italics.

*In view of the above, and the client's more general concern to protect the local environment, specific site rules will be developed to limit contract activities and entry into or through these areas.*

*Demolition and general clearance of buildings within the site has already been completed by the client. The client does not, however, have any record or information on the long-term previous history of the site or its land usage.*

**An area of contaminated land has been identified on the site. The following issues have been considered:**

- **direct health risk to workers on site**
- **neighbours affected by contaminated dust**
- **failure of structural elements due to contact with aggressive environment.**

*A separate advance contract will be let prior to progress of construction work. Removal, transportation and disposal of the contaminated ground is to be undertaken in a controlled manner during this advance contract.*

**The site is located in a heavily developed area. The effects of the following items need to be specifically considered during construction:**

- **noise**
- **vibration**
- **dust**

**on occupiers of adjacent buildings which are of the following categories:**

- **domestic residential buildings**
- **commercial/industrial properties**
- **public buildings - schools, hospitals, old peoples' homes.**

**The following points are noted:**

- **Domestic residential properties are situated approximately 10m from the site boundary.**

- **A small industrial estate is adjacent to the site. One factory unit has a glass sulphur containment vessel which is sensitive to vibration.**

- **No public building is adjacent to the site, although an infant and junior school is within the general locality. Security of the construction site is a necessary consideration, particularly where children are concerned.**

**Some older residential properties are constructed on a gravel-type material. Foundations of these buildings are expected to be corbeled brickwork or stone. Excessive vibration adjacent to these properties could cause consolidation of the gravel and the subsequent loss of foundations to buildings.**

**Disused mine workings have been identified in the area. They are sufficiently remote to be unaffected by construction, although excessive ground vibration could cause localised collapse.**

**Vehicle access has to be maintained:**

- **for workers and emergency vehicles at the two factory units**
- **along adjacent public highways**
- **at the roundabouts on each end of the scheme.**

Existing statutory undertakers' apparatus is present on or adjacent to the site:

- gas - main on site but unaffected by work
- water - diversion required
- telecommunications - diversion required
- electricity - overhead wires require diversion
  - underground cable on site but unaffected by work
  - substation with switch gear requiring protection from dust and vibration
- street lighting
- fire hydrants - the existing hydrants, which are to remain, must be kept unobstructed and access free.

*The statutory undertakers will complete diversion work to all existing services in advance of any work required on the main contract.*

Methane gas has been detected on the site and can be carried by local groundwater.

Temporary ground excavations, permanent drainage runs, manholes or interceptors may contain methane gas. Vented manhole and interceptor covers are provided to drainage systems.

## 3. Existing drawings

The following drawings are included for information:

- existing statutory undertakers' apparatus
- mine workings detail.

There are no existing drawings available for the foundations of demolished buildings.

## 4. The design

Vehicular and public rights of way are present within or immediately adjacent to the site. Conflict between construction and these rights of way is thought likely at:

- the roundabouts where the scheme ties into the existing road network
- accesses to factory units
- local side roads adjacent to the site.

The soils investigation identified:

- poor ground conditions and predicted difficulty in constructing open excavations in restricted areas. This is one of the reasons for the specification of contiguous pile construction on that part of the retaining wall adjacent to the factory accesses

- a low acceptable ground bearing pressure. Use of a trough design achieved the low ground pressures/stresses necessary, while still providing the required height of retaining wall.

The groundwater table throughout the site is just below structure foundation level. This has been taken into account when considering the stability of any structure founded within this soil.

- the soils investigation report will be included within the tender documentation.

Specification of auger replacement contiguous piles has been made, taking account of the:

- noise levels
- structural integrity of glass sulphur containment vessel within an adjacent factory unit
- consolidation of gravels beneath property foundations
- structural integrity of disused mine workings.

A possible construction sequence has been identified for trough construction which highlights the importance of various elements related to collapse during construction and maintenance:

- Pile Capping beam - ties the top of all discrete piles together
- Centre Beam - provides structural rigidity and stability
- Road Pavement - acts as prop to the piles
- Thrust block - transfers prop force into piles.

Refer to drawings and specifications for full details.

A detailed construction statement and method sequence, including calculations and drawings, will be required from the contractor. Measures to deal with noise and dust are to be included in method statement.

The seepage of bentonite type material into mine workings, ducts and services is possible.

Contamination of watercourses from run-off during earthwork operations must be contained.

## 5. Construction materials

The following construction materials have particular health risks:

- Paint systems - solvent-based paint system specified, special precautions necessary
- Joint sealants and sealing compounds - these have not been specified. The construction and material details will need to be agreed with the engineer.

The COSHH Regulations should be taken into account.

## 6. Site wide elements

*Site access and egress points have been identified by the client in agreement with the Local Authority, Police and Environmental Services Department. The specification requires the effects of site traffic on the local environment and upon the people living and working in the area to be kept to a minimum.*

*Site security has been addressed within the specification with a requirement for fencing and out-of-work-hours security patrols. Public relations should also be actively developed by the site management team.*

*The client will assist in this respect through the local residents' groups formed to obtain local input into the general development plans.*

*Location and maintenance of temporary site accommodation.*

*Location and maintenance of materials storage, plant and unloading areas.*

Vehicular and public rights of way are present within the site. Conflict between construction and these rights of way may occur at:

- **roundabouts where the scheme ties into the existing road network**
- **accesses to factory units**
- **local side roads adjacent to the site.**

## 7. Overlap with client's undertaking

*The following points of possible conflict are identified with the client's undertaking:*

- *with statutory undertakers carrying out diversion of apparatus*
- *with contractors completing accommodation work on the nearby residential properties*
- *with contractor completing contaminated ground remediation.*

*It is envisaged that these items of work will be completed prior to commencement of the main contract. However, if in the event this is not the case, it is considered that these elements of work will not affect the main contract and that these areas of the site can be effectively isolated until completed.*

## 8. Site Rules

*Specific points identified for adoption with site rules.*

*Construction noise:*

- *limit times of working*
- *level of noise.*

## 9. Continuing liaison

*The following is identified for continuing liaison between parties:*

- *Contractor to submit his design elements for packages to the planning supervisor.*

- *Contractor to submit substantial design changes arising from unforeseen eventualities during project execution to the planning supervisor and designer.*

## 10.7 THE HEALTH AND SAFETY FILE

Items for inclusion by the planning supervisor within the health and safety file have been identified by the designer throughout progression of the design. These health and safety issues are highlighted below as the contributions from the designer to the planning supervisor.

- Details of the structures equipment and maintenance facilities:

  1. Drainage interceptors
  2. Drainage access and maintenance details

- Details of location and nature of utilities and services

  1. Fire Hydrant Locations

- General details of construction methods and materials

1. Trough construction sequence highlighting the importance of various elements, particularly with regard to the sequence of any future demolition.

In addition to the above, the designer will submit the following documents for inclusion with the file:

- Soils Report
- Soil and Groundwater Analysis
- Design Criteria and Assumptions.

# 11  Tunnel project

## 11.1  INTRODUCTION

This example of design development, incorporating the requirements of the proposed Regulations, is based on an actual project. The example applies, in outline, regulation 13 to part of a complex sewerage system that includes tunnels, pipelines, pumping stations and a major sewage treatment works, and will attempt to focus on the design development considerations required for the tunnel section. The exact route is not identified as this is a local matter not relevant to the example.

The design is progressed through three stages:

• concept
• outline
• detailed.

Other parts of this £100 million project will be complementary and create interface considerations. These design packages have been undertaken by a number of designers and the only common denominator is the client. It is not part of this example to comment on the planning supervisor's duty to ensure that designers pay adequate regard to, co-operate and co-ordinate their activities, but it is acknowledged that this is a crucial and important role.

The author wishes to emphasise that the design was completed prior to the publication of the proposed Regulations. The example given is therefore based on the author's interpretation of designers' probable response to the Regulations.

## 11.2  PROJECT INFORMATION

### 11.2.1  Purpose

The project was designed to replace an existing sewage outfall system by the construction of a flow transfer system and sewage treatment works, thus enabling the client to comply with the EC Directives on bathing waters and urban wastewater treatment.

### 11.2.2  Scope

The scope of work comprises:

• construction of 9km of 2.44m diameter gravity tunnel

• two stormwater pumping stations/screening plants with maximum approximate discharges of $6m^3$/sec and $5m^3$/sec respectively

• construction of a stormwater outfall to serve one of the new pumping stations

• construction of two pumping stations of 815 l/sec and 162 l/sec installed capacity

• 2km sewer connections of variable diameter to tunnel shafts

- construction of 4.3km of 300mm and 900mm diameter pumping mains

plus associated works.

The principal element of this project is the 9km long, 2.44m diameter tunnel - the subject of this example.

### 11.2.3   Location

The project location is in the south west of England and includes three major population centres.

### 11.2.4   Client requirements and local environment

The client requires a scheme which will transfer sewage flows and contain stormwater, allowing it to be pumped at a controlled rate into a new treatment works.  The tunnel will be constructed beneath a highly populated residential area which relies heavily on the tourist trade as its principal source of income.  The tunnel section will run under residential and commercial properties.  There are road and rail services in the area as well as the existing services.  Restrictions on highway works apply during peak holiday periods.  Therefore, the scheme must be constructed with minimal disruption to the residents and minimal environmental disturbance or impact.

The client accepts clear accountability for ensuring safety and health are properly considered during the design and construction processes.

The client is also mindful of the potential costs imposed on construction work due to unplanned events and is determined to prevent such unnecessary costs being imposed on their customers.

## 11.3  CONCEPT DESIGN STAGE

### 11.3.1   Discussion of health and safety issues

*Appointment of planning supervisor*

Regulation 6(3) requires clients to appoint a planning supervisor as soon as is practicable once they have sufficient information etc. to make this appointment.  The concept design involved many specialist consultants.  Consequently, clients may decide to appoint a planning supervisor for this strategic stage, whether or not the role is given to another for the design stages per se.

*The principal hazards identified*

These include:

- uncertain geological conditions
- deep excavations
- underground working
- contaminated ground
- ingress of gas causing fire or explosion
- lack of oxygen
- sudden and unforeseen ingress of water
- loss of compressed air from workings
- effect on overground structures.

*Initial assessment of the 'severity of the hazards'*

Is this work routine and are the hazards clearly understood by the design team?

Will the work be undertaken by a sufficiently experienced and competent contractor?

Designers must assume that the client will only permit tenders from experienced and competent contractors (regulation 8).

The designer should review the level of available knowledge of hazard and risk assessment, drawing on specialist expertise where applicable, i.e. if the designer does not employ a 'competent' health and safety practitioner (see regulation 6 of *Management of Health and Safety at Work Regulations 1992*). For the purposes of this example, it should be noted that the designer has its own in-house health and safety expertise, has also engaged an external health and safety consultancy and that the client will operate a selective tender list.

*Review of possible design solutions for the Scheme taking into account the hazards and issues in accordance with good risk assessment protocol*

The review of possible design solutions incorporates (among many other considerations) the assessment of hazards to health and safety.

The preliminary study indicated that there were 27 possible sites with approximately 130 scheme options available. Studies revealed that there were problems with many of the possible sites due to environmental, economic, technical and health and safety difficulties.

Consequently, a short list of five was selected. Two of these were discounted on health and safety considerations following detailed investigations. These indicated that severely contaminated ground may exist due to their former use as landfill or gas works facilities.

Of the 130 possible options available, it was realised at an early stage that there were only two practical possibilities for the transfer of sewage from one major population centre to the other:

1. tunnel transfer with storage provided within the volume of the interceptor, or

2. pumped pipeline with isolated stormwater storage.

The tunnel option was preferred since it minimised public disruption and environmental impact. Subsidiary decisions on tunnel construction included the choice of compressed air versus atmospheric operations. In the interests of health and safety, atmospheric working was the preferred option at this stage.

Having settled on the location and preferred option, the designer would then carry out more detailed Hazard and Operability Study and Risk Assessments (HAZOPRA).

The designer should provide information for the health and safety file, and record any significant information, e.g. unusual or abnormal ground conditions, contamination or leachate, and initiate the health and safety plan.

## 11.3.2 Designer's contribution to the health and safety plan

The health and safety issues identified at the concept design stage which will need consideration are listed below:

*The design issues*

The 2.44m diameter tunnel, 9km in length, is to be constructed under a heavily populated seaside resort area. The work is to be carried out with minimum environmental disturbance, taking into account traffic and visitor levels that are greatly increased during the peak summer months.

*Route selection*

The selection of appropriate routes for the interceptor tunnel was based on the following principal criteria:

- Interception of sewers

  Connection of the existing sewerage system to the tunnel will occur at strategic points within the catchment. At each sewerage connection shaft the health and safety considerations required that the sewerage works should be minimised as far as possible, and connection works to the tunnel should take place with minimum disruption to traffic and that shafts are readily accessible for maintenance purposes.

- Minimisation of disruption

  The tunnel route has been selected to avoid passing beneath buildings, thus minimising the effects of settlement on residential or commercial properties. Routing to follow public highways where possible to reduce the risk to properties, but this increases the risk of damage to utility services in the highway.

- Identification of suitable drive sites

  Due to the geology of the subject area, it is proposed to split the 9km tunnel into three drives of differing ground conditions. Selection of the route of each drive was influenced by the location of suitable land areas for a large diameter drive shaft. Health and safety considerations for the main drive shaft sites were:

    - size of site
    - position relative to properties
    - position relative to highway network
    - position relative to suitable spoil disposal site.

- Geological conditions

  The engineering and economic feasibility of the tunnel route had to be established as early as possible. Geotechnical considerations will directly affect construction methods and hence the health and safety implications of the project. Following a comprehensive desk study of the geology along possible routes, including an assessment of potential construction sites, a small physical and geophysical scale reconnaissance was commissioned to establish preliminary geotechnical information.

  This allowed basic assumptions to be made about the methods of working, type of spoil, rates of progress and areas of contaminated land to be avoided by the tunnel operations.

- Access for construction

  Preliminary access arrangements for the construction of the tunnel, number of access points, provisional locations of shafts, connections etc. were established. At this stage these are considered preliminary, but it is hoped that only minor alterations will be needed following more detailed ground investigations.

Because of the construction of the shafts and tunnels, the ground conditions are considered to be major hazards. These will be the focus of the remainder of the example.

*Compressed air*

The health and safety plan assumes at this stage that the work will be carried out at atmospheric pressure. The need for compressed air working may arise, dependent on the detailed ground investigation reports. In view of this, a subsidiary health and safety plan is being developed in reserve. This subsidiary plan is not included in this example.

*Main access to the tunnel*

The horizontal spacing of access shafts to the main tunnel was a significant issue during the concept design stage. Requirements to construct sewer interception points within the catchment dictated that shafts were generally spaced at not more than 500m centres. Local circumstances in some areas dictated locations of shafts which exceeded 700-800m spacing. Research was carried out to determine the maximum permissible spacing between man-access points for a tunnel of this size to allow for safe working practices during routine maintenance. Investigation quickly established that there is no statutory requirement and no approved code of practice for this element of design. Information from similar tunnelling projects indicated that the shaft spacing was pragmatic, based on the client's own policy or on what was perceived as good engineering practice from other tunnelling projects.

A simplified risk assessment was carried out at the concept design stage which indicated that a maximum shaft spacing of 500m would enable escape from the tunnel within the limitations imposed by 10-minute emergency air packs. Where the tunnel is constructed to a curved alignment the maximum distance is reduced. Additionally, where sewer interception shafts are spaced at 700-800m, intermediate man-access shafts, solely for access purposes, were proposed. Marker signs will be placed at 25m intervals giving distances to the nearest intermediate shaft.

Preliminary indications should be given for the location of existing power supplies, pipelines, underground streams, sewers etc.

### 11.3.3   Health and safety file

The health and safety file was started at the concept design stage. This is intended to contain significant information for reliable performance of competent contractors, operators, maintenance staff or demolition contractors from a health and safety standpoint, e.g. unusual or abnormal ground conditions, contamination or leachates. It also provides a record should the scheme be shelved and re-started.

Significant information gained along the tunnel route at concept design stage included:

- topography and surface survey
- geology
- hydrology
- old workings
- borehole results
- results of groundwater tests
- underground survey results
- explosive or toxic gases.

Having obtained this information, risk assessments would be carried out and significant risks identified. Only the information regarding these risks needs to be included in the file, e.g. the possible ingress of explosive or toxic gases. Other items included in the health and safety file are preliminary design drawings and/or sketches. As more than one designer is involved in the project, each should keep their own health and safety information and make these available to the planning supervisor.

## 11.4 OUTLINE DESIGN STAGE

### 11.4.1 Discussion of health and safety issues

*Examination of scheme options*

At this stage the major issues concerned with the proposed tunnel are:

- establishment of detailed ground investigation information
- tunnelling methods
- effects of tunnelling operations on overlying properties
- shaft sinking
- safe access and egress
- safe access for future maintenance and repair
- emergency procedures both during construction and subsequent operation.

*Method of construction*

Outline solutions were proposed for tunnel construction. After examining the options, it was determined that the preferred method would be by means of a tunnel boring machine working at atmospheric pressure. The other options - 'drill and blast' and 'roadheader' - were rejected on grounds which did not raise safe working issues. All the assumptions made at this stage will be subject to the results of detailed ground investigations which are currently being undertaken.

*Tunnel routes*

Tunnel route options were examined in more detail. Whilst it was intended to link each site in a direct line, a number of factors were taken into account. Contaminated ground from an old gas works caused the tunnel route to be moved further inland.

The effect of construction and possible settlement on adjacent properties restricted the route as far as reasonably practicable to areas of low property density, ideally beneath highways and parklands.

An assessment of the likely effect of tunnelling operations on properties and buildings overlying the tunnel was made, based on the results of the preliminary ground investigation. This resulted in the production of preliminary 'zone of influence' drawings which indicate areas containing properties at higher and lower risk of settlement due to tunnel construction. While it is intended that ground movement will be strictly limited in the design specification, zone of influence drawings give an indication of the risk relating to variable geological conditions. They will continue to be developed as knowledge of ground conditions increases.

Shaft location considerations took into account local access and services. Excavation depths were kept to a minimum wherever possible by utilising low ground level and the need to pick up existing sewers. This latter goal was made more difficult by the design specification to keep the shaft covers a minimum of 4.5m above ordnance datum (AOD) in order to accommodate the maximum surcharge level from peak flows in the finished project.

The design solutions to meet these criteria restricted the choice of site locations, particularly in the western area. Taking all the factors into consideration, the final route option allows for good, clear safe access and egress, not only during construction but also during the subsequent maintenance.

*Construction strategy*

Construction strategy next had to be considered. A 9km tunnel is a major project by any standards and therefore a whole range of options were examined and discarded. The final decision would affect some of the design considerations in terms of health and safety. In addition, there are practical economic and contractual reasons to be considered. Having examined the options, the designer recommended that the works should be let in three separate contracts of 3,829m, 1,739m and 3,483m respectively. This recommendation was influenced by geological, economic, programming and practical construction criteria. The contract strategy for tunnelling operations has yet to be determined by the client.

Taking the requirement of the CDM Regulations into account, the above recommendation has the disadvantage from a health and safety aspect of creating a number of contract interfaces. Where independent contractors are appointed it would increase the numbers involved in meeting the requirement of regulation 9 of the *Management of Health and Safety at Work Regulations 1992*. It would also increase the work involved in preparing the construction stage health and safety plan(s). Designers will need to be aware of the client's intentions in respect of the planning supervisor appointment. If, as is almost certain, significant design takes place after main construction contracts are let, the planning supervisor duties would apply to all incomplete design (apart from contractors' temporary works) and interactions between design elements will have to be resolved. It would seem logical for a lead designer to take on board the planning supervisor role, providing he has the 'competence' to do so.

The risk of flooding and ingress of gases during construction will have to be addressed on the basis of these decisions.

*Maintenance*

The risk of ingress of gases should be borne in mind before entering tunnels for maintenance.

## 11.4.2 Designer's contribution to the health and safety plan

The health and safety issues identified at the outline design stage which will need consideration by the designer for the plan are discussed below.

Where the hazard and risk are significant but there is no beneficial design solution, the plan will indicate to the planning supervisor the need for proper provision, but will leave the 'how' to the expertise of the subsequent contractor. The designer should be careful not to erode contractors' responsibilities and compromise the client commercially by over-detailing the systems of work to be adopted.

The following hazards and risks have been identified and assessed and need further consideration at this stage:

*Emergencies*

- ground collapse at the face with possible inrush of water
- failure of temporary or permanent support some distance behind the face, with possible inrush of water
- flooding in the tunnel from the face, from burst water pipes, sewers, or pumping failure
- gas and explosion
- oxygen deficiency
- fires
- accidents from moving plant
- plant and power failure
- sabotage.

*Explosives*

- pre-blast surveys will be undertaken to assess the character and structure of the geological strata and the effects on underground services

- provision for an adequate, secure explosive reserve station

- explosives to be transported to site safely and securely in a properly constructed mine car in accordance with the approved Code of Practice

- only trained supervisors and operatives to be employed

- set procedures to be clearly defined and communicated to all personnel.

*Drop shafts*

- Excavation

  The method of excavation and support of the drop shafts will be determined by the ground and groundwater conditions at each shaft site. The studies carried out at outline design stage indicate:

  - pre-cast segmented concrete lining with watertight gaskets as the best design solution

  - other contractor proposed systems may be appropriate; therefore, the final decision may be dependent on the ground conditions (which may be different for each shaft); will be decided after consideration of the working method and method statements of tendering contractors.

- Shaft environment

  Preliminary considerations at this stage in the health and safety plan include:

  - use of explosives confined to pre-determined time windows to minimise noise and environmental nuisance

  - site layout in the neighbourhood of each shaft specifically to take into account lay-down areas, plant operations, muck removal, skip movements, etc.

  - off-site vehicular movements at pre-determined times and by pre-determined traffic routes to authorised and supervised disposal sites with public safety being the paramount consideration.

Design solutions include enclosure construction, sound proofing, dust minimisation and temporary ground support systems. Ring segment transport and support system, particularly where hand building is required, may be designed in outline, subject to proposals by competing contractors and to the designer's acceptance of the preferred contractor's method statements.

*Public safety*

Tendering contractors will be asked to explain their proposed arrangements for ensuring public safety, including preventing entry by unauthorised persons, vehicles and plant movements, noise and dust suppression, and for liaising with local residents' associations and keeping the client informed.

### 11.4.3 Designer's contribution to the health and safety file

Information on the materials to be used and the system adopted to support the permanent works should be entered in the file. In addition, any unusual design detail that may affect future work in terms of risk should be recorded.

As detailed ground investigations proceed, the information in the file requires updating and amending. It is essential that old and redundant information is removed , e.g. inaccurate geological data superseded by the detailed investigation.

It may also be prudent for the designer to include information on the Control of Substances Hazardous to Health (COSHH) and assessments of the risk. Particular attention must be given to COSHH associated with tunnel boring methods and muck-pass systems, as well as drop shaft construction operations.

## 11.5 DETAILED DESIGN STAGE

### 11.5.1 Discussion of health and safety issues

#### *Flexibility of design approach*

Most of the design options have been considered and either adapted, discarded or closed off. It is better to be flexible as, no matter how expert the design team, the contractor(s) must have the freedom to suggest improvements and to be responsible for safety management when carrying out the work.

The health and safety plan now begins to address significant hazards and those identified at the outline design stage with a view to avoiding or reducing these, taking into account the other design considerations. Any special forms of control required during the construction phase should feature in the plan.

The issues and hazards considered at the detailed design stage will take into account design interface risks. The scheme will involve a sewerage agent as the designer of some of the feeder pipelines and subsidiary works. The CDM Regulations place the responsibility upon the planning supervisor to ensure that these designs also pay adequate regard to health and safety issues and deal with awkward (health and safety) interactions.

#### *Review of each section, site or phase*

Design management, whether or not quality assured, provides for design reviews often by peer groups. Ways in which designers have responded to regulation 13 - adequacy, interactions between responses, and the assessment of the health and safety plan - can be taken into these reviews. These should be minuted to provide a record of the action taken. Planning supervisors should be told of the programme, have the right to attend any review and receive minutes of each review whether or not they have attended that session.

Detailed consideration can add to hazards identified in the previous health and safety stage plans, for example:

- unexpected or unusual tasks
- ventilation
- emergency systems
- escape routes
- temporary support systems
- temporary lighting and power systems
- methods of work
- precautions to be taken to protect workforce
- signalling systems

- control of entry
- welfare.

Construction methods and programme - review:

- health and safety plan to date
- design solution to health and safety risks
- resulting construction sequences and methods.

Maintenance, repair and renovation:

- review access and ventilation
- permanent safety features
- gas monitoring and oxygen deficiency systems
- emergency evacuation systems and life support systems
- permanent sign requirements
- security.

Review the health and safety file input.

## 11.5.2   Development of the health and safety plan

The skeleton plan, outlined at the concept design stage, is beginning to take final shape. Design solutions have been applied as far as is reasonably practicable. The purpose at this stage is finally to identify the significant risks that tendering contractors will need to take into account when delivering their bids.

The CDM Regulations require the appointment of a principal contractor and it will be his responsibility, among others, to develop the pre-tender stage plan.

### *Nature of project*

The plan for the scheme will include information on:

- nature of project
- existing environment
- existing drawings
- the design
- construction materials
- site wide elements
- overlap with client's undertaking
- site rules
- continuing liaison.

### *Design*

Hazard analysis and risk assessment have identified the significant risks to the health and safety of persons employed on the construction works and to persons affected by those works. Where the risks are identified as generic and inherent in construction work of this nature, and well-documented solutions apply (e.g. edge protection, excavation support, COSHH procedures etc.), the plan will make a simple reference that these are the responsibility of the principal contractor and other contractors. It can be assumed that they are competent and adequately resourced to discharge their health and safety responsibilities.

Where an assessment identifies special hazards where standard solutions do not apply, the health and safety plan will outline these so that tendering contractors can plan and provide for them. For especially problematic work, the preferred contractor will be required to produce, and justify, method statements before appointment. Exceptionally, consultants may provide method statements as illustrations of how the work may be done: contractors will be responsible for the chosen method.

### Shaft design

The method of shaft excavation and support will be determined by the ground and groundwater conditions at each shaft site.

As the water table is close to ground surface at most shaft sites, the preferred construction is by use of pre-cast, segmental concrete lining with water tight gaskets.

The contractor may, however, consider alternatives involving shotcrete, mesh, lattice arches with secondary linings or other methods.

It is envisaged that various methods of construction will be involved, with excavation using explosive, drilling and raised boring.

The three main access shafts will be excavated in preparation for the tunnel works.

The special hazards identified which the contractor will be required to address in the health and safety plan are:

- sudden inrush of water
- possibility of drainage related subsidence to overground properties
- removal of spoil
- noise reduction measures
- temporary support ground where raised bored method is used
- excavation of spoil via muck pass into the tunnel
- the effect of muck pass on the programme and its possible restriction on early tunnel ventilation and pumping
- the health effects of diesel exhaust fumes from locomotives hauling rail muck cars.

The above are only indicators of some of the potential hazards to be addressed at the detailed design stage and a typical detail for an off-line shaft is shown in Figure 18.

### Tunnel design

The special hazards identified for which the contractor will be required to produce sub-plans (sometimes referred to as method statements or site specific procedures) are:

- emergency evacuation procedures
- explosives
- compressed air working
- design of temporary support works
- radiation sources
- flood protection measures
- false work support systems
- ventilation systems
- tunnel driving, spoil removal and segment lining operations
- welfare
- commissioning

plus others, as requested by the client at contract stage.

The risks from generic and inherent hazards, although subject to clearly understood solutions, are

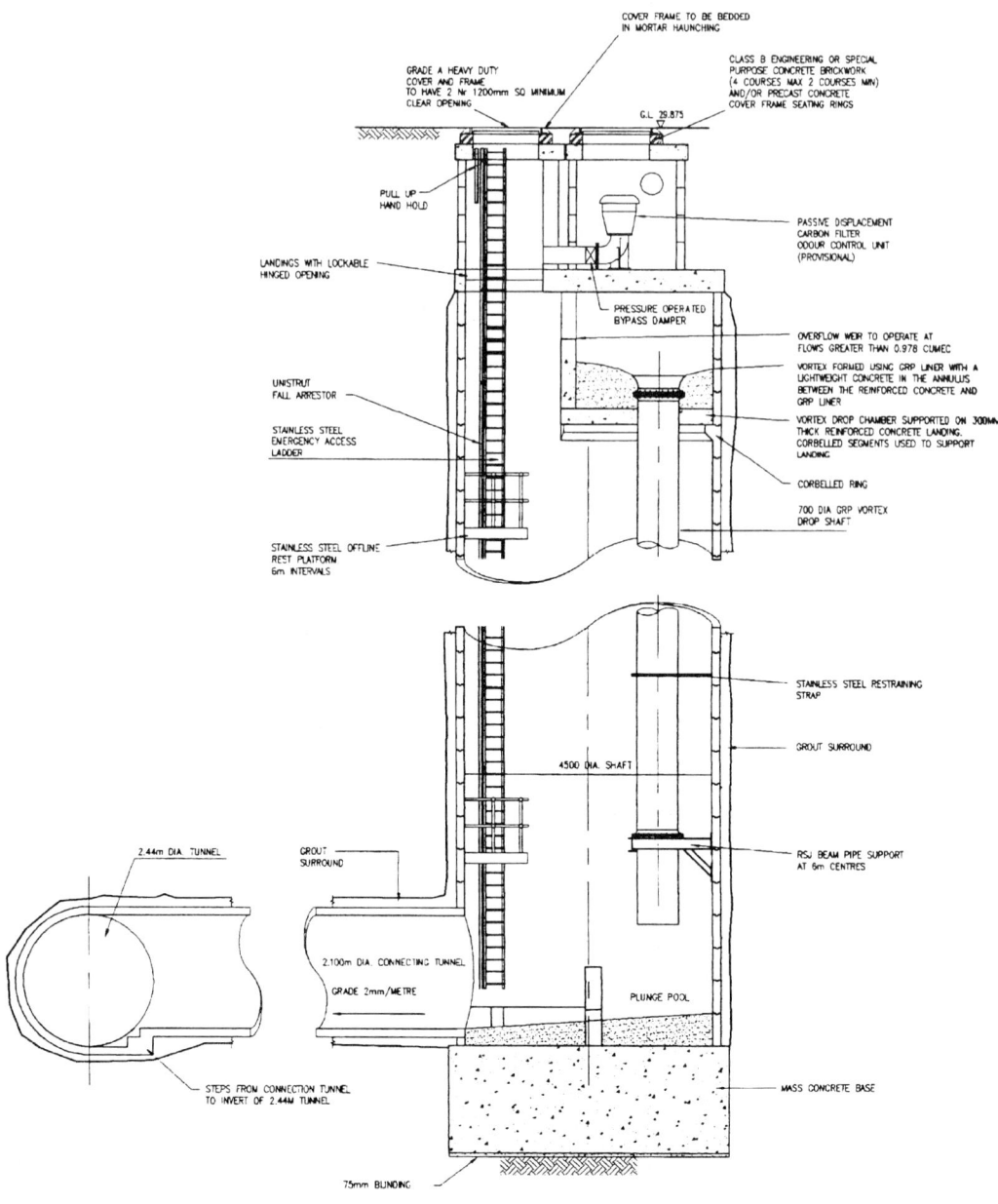

**Figure 18** *Detail of typical off-line shaft*

only minimised if effective controls are managed and implemented by the responsible contractor. These include, but are not limited to:

- falls from heights
- materials or objects falling
- temporary working platforms
- overhead power lines
- buried services
- restricted access and egress
- noise
- dust and fumes
- site plant
- temporary electricity supplies
- diving operations
- liquefied petroleum gas

- scaffolding
- site security.

The design implementation and management of safe methods of work are the responsibility of contractors, each of whom may be assumed to be competent and adequately resourced (regulations 6 and 8).

### Construction materials

All contractors may be assumed to know and comply with the *Control of Substances Hazardous to Health Regulations 1989* (COSHH). Designers, however, can remove or reduce these hazards when selecting or specifying articles and substances. These include, but are not be restricted to:

- grouts
- adhesives
- coatings
- paint finishes
- linings
- additives etc.

When special precautions additional to those a competent contractor would take are required, they should be noted in the health and safety plan.

## 11.5.3 Designer's contribution to the health and safety file

Input the necessary information to the file:

- final ground condition survey reports
- detail as-built design drawings
- COSHH assessments
- risk assessments
- noise assessments
- diving inspection reports
- details of articles and substances used in construction
- M & E drawings
- HAZOP studies and risk assessments
- any other information which competent contractors need to be told so that they can estimate and plan for maintenance and repair.

There are two aspects to health and safety file.

First, designers may wish to maintain a record of health and safety information for their own reference, e.g. investigations, risk assessments, decisions made on health and safety factors, records of peer reviews, information that a future operator will need, such as principles of structural design, escape routes, emergency procedures, control systems, contaminated ground and the like.

Second, the planning supervisor will need information from the designer to contribute to the health and safety file to pass to the client on completion of the project. This information will enable those who may wish to work on the completed project to:

- access the plant
- operate the system
- maintain, service, modify or extend the system
- plan for and respond to emergencies

in a safe manner.

## 11.6 THE CIVIL ENGINEER'S CONTRIBUTION TO THE PRE-TENDER STAGE HEALTH AND SAFETY PLAN*

### 1.     Nature of project

Client:                          **Waste Water Disposal Ltd (WWDL)**

The construction work:           **Construction of a complex sewerage system that includes tunnels, pipelines, pumping stations, outfalls and a 9km 2.44m diameter tunnel to which this plan applies.**

**The tunnel will be constructed employing traditional tunnel boring methods and segmented concrete rings with associated shafts and ancillary works.**

**All work to be carried out at atmospheric pressure.**

Timescale for completion
of construction:                 **Two years**

### 2.     The existing environment

Variable ground conditions under highly populated area.

- **route of tunnel**
- *identification of existing services*
- *existing traffic systems and restrictions*
- **traffic routes for spoil disposal**
- **traffic routes for construction material delivery**
- **delivery windows**
- **water table**
- **contaminated ground**
- **public and private water abstraction boreholes**
- *underground services*
- *underground streams*
- **toxic or explosive gas.**

An Environmental Impact Assessment would have been carried out at the start of the project.

### 3.     Existing drawings of sewers and pipelines

- *to be provided by sewerage agent*
- *water services to be provided by client*
- *electricity supplies to be provided by statutory authority*
- *gas supply pipelines to be provided by statutory authority.*

### 4.     The design

- **Areas of hazardous and contaminated ground are known to exist at several points along the route. Extensive landfill operations have occurred during past development and the fill material is as yet unidentified.**

---

* In this example plan, the case study designer's inputs to the plan are shown in bold face, while the inputs of the others are shown in italics.

- **Site survey and analysis reports attached.**

- *The principal contractor will be required to detail his intended system of work and the safety plan requirements.*

- *The principal contractor will be responsible for ensuring the information is made available to the competent contractor.*

- **The designer will identify those specific problems arising from the structural design which will be outside a competent contractor's experience. This will include particular health and safety hazards arising from access or sequencing.**

- *It will be the responsibility of any competent contractor to detail its proposals for managing these problems and inserting them into the health and safety plan prior to work commencing on site, namely:*

  - *ventilation*
  - *emergency procedures*
  - *escape routes*
  - *temporary support systems*
  - *temporary power and lighting systems*
  - *precautions to protect the workforce*
  - *control of entry*
  - *control of moving plant.*

## 5.    Construction materials

- **The designer will design out, as far as is reasonably practicable, hazardous materials with a view to minimising or removing hazards.**

- *The principal contractor will be responsible for their own COSHH assessments and for implementing adequate control measures.*

## 6.    Site wide elements

- Noise

*Noise is to be kept within limits specified in the Noise at Work Regulations using best known suppression methods.*

*The principal contractor will liaise with the Environmental Health Officer and provide noise assessments and establish control measures. These are to be incorporated into the health and safety plan.*

- Security of sites

**The principal contractor will be responsible for maintaining all sites in a secure state. All areas are to be fenced in accordance with Health and Safety Executive's Guidance Note GS7.**

**The principal contractor will ensure that only authorised persons are permitted within site areas and will implement a proper authorisation procedure and controls.**

- **The principal contractor will ensure strict adherence to the pre-determined traffic routes, delivery time and restrictions identified by the designer in consultation with the local highways department.**

- *Welfare facilities.*

## 7. Overlap with client's undertakings

*In terms of the tunnel scheme, there will be interfaces with existing sewers. The designer has minimised these but the principal contractor will be required to produce a method statement for insertion into the health and safety plan.*

## 8. Site Rules

These include:

- *safety inspections and audits*
- *responsibilities*
- *permit to work systems*
- *training of all staff*
- *protective clothing and equipment*
- *restricted access*
- *testing.*

## 9. Continuing liaison

**The Resident Engineer (RE) will co-ordinate regular progress meetings between the designer, WWD Ltd and the principal contractor. These meetings will examine health and safety issues arising from design changes, including control systems, accident investigations, amendments to the health and safety plan, information for the health and safety file.**

**The RE will ensure weekly health and safety meetings are held to co-ordinate the activities of all contractors, WWD Ltd and the County Council and Borough Council's highways and Environmental health departments. These meetings will be subject to a formal agenda and minuted to record corrective actions.**

**In cases of disagreement with the client in respect of interpretation of the statutory requirements, WWD's view will prevail and the Resident Engineer will monitor standards accordingly.**

## 11.7 THE HEALTH AND SAFETY FILE

Items for inclusion in the health and safety file have been identified during the various development phases of the design sequence.

These include, where they have a significant reference to health and safety of construction, operation or maintenance:

- geology
- hydrology
- old workings
- underground survey results in respect of explosive or toxic gases
- contaminated ground
- construction materials
- substances hazardous to health
- detail of shaft and tunnel connections

- detail of fire equipment and emergency rescue locations
- preliminary maintenance information
- set of current drawings.

The health and safety file should only contain information which is significant and relevant to the ongoing health and safety requirements during future construction, operation and maintenance operations.

Information, such as risk assessments of substances hazardous to health, generated as part of the construction phase, medical surveillance results etc. are the proper province of the employers concerned. Records which must be kept by responsible employers should not be placed in the project file.

# 12 Issues raised by the study

## 12.1 GENERAL

This report reflects the signed and published CDM Regulations and accompanying Approved Code of Practice, although the majority of the drafting was carried out against a background of continuing discussion on the final form of the Regulations and the ACOP.

Some of the issues raised by the study and the opinion of the Project Steering Group on these matters are set out below.

## 12.2 ISSUES

### 12.2.1 Risk assessment

The Management of Health and Safety at Work Regulations 1992 introduced a formal requirement for assessments of risk to be carried out so that measures necessary to comply with health and safety law could be identified. This applied to all industries and much of the advice [1,2,3,4] has been written with the workplaces of manufacturing industry in mind rather than construction sites. Contractors, however, have endeavoured for many years to apply the principles of risk assessment to make construction sites safer and designers of civil engineering and building works have made general assessments in a subjective manner.

The new element introduced by the CDM Regulations and the ACOP is the responsibility on designers to make risk assessment an integral part of the design function when decisions are being taken regarding the balance between aesthetic, technical, financial or other aspects and the health and safety of construction workers. The ACOP paragraph 60 states that "as the design develops, the designer needs to examine methods by which the structure might be built and analyse the hazards and risks associated with these methods in the context of his design choices."

The problem for designers is that the ability to make comparative risk assessments requires a knowledge of construction processes which not all possess. At present, the expectation is that most situations will require a structured, but basically qualitative approach and the advice available in *Designing for health and safety in construction* is written for that level of analysis. This approach will usually satisfy legal requirements. However, complex construction projects may well require a more quantitative approach and for these the procedures presented in the literature[1,2,3,4] will need to be developed and refined. For example, that the notion of time or frequency be introduced into the concept of the probability of a hazard causing harm.

Generic responses to design problems in relation to site health and safety will be developed. It is anticipated that situations that experience has shown to cause trouble will be looked at by designers in the balance of design considerations with the help of possible solutions.

---

1 *Five steps to risk assessment*, HSE 1994
2 *Principles of Health and Safety at Work*, A St J Holt and H Andrews, IOSH 1992
3 *Risk assessment - a practical guide*, The Safety & Health Practitioners, IOSH, May 1993
4 *Successful health and safety management* [HS(G)65], HSE 1991

It is important to remember that designers are not required to contemplate every eventual site risk, but only to consider those that reasonably can be foreseen at the time of design. At concept and feasibility stage much may be able to be done in general terms by avoiding or minimising dangers of the site environment, easing problems of access, etc. In some cases, at later stages, the detail in design may in effect specify a work method.

Competence of the appointed contractors can be assumed; but familiarity of contractors with a task merely affects the weight given to the avoidance or reduction of the risks in the balance of design considerations: it does not remove the need to consider it. In the case studies, the phrases "safety boundary" and "routinely safely carried out" refer to operations which have been considered by the designer and judged to fall within the abilities of a competent contractor.

## 12.2.2  The health and safety aspects of the operation of facilities

The CDM Regulations are applicable only to projects involving "construction work or cleaning work", based on the definitions given in regulation 2. This includes work in connection with the construction, maintenance, repair and demolition of the works.

Operation is a completely separate function from maintenance, although in some cases the distinction may not be immediately clear, for example in respect of some items of mechanical and electrical plant. In other cases it is much more clear cut.

> Example: A bridge is used to cross an obstacle. The design of the bridge such that it is safe to use is no concern of the CDM Regulations. Aspects of the design that relate to maintenance, e.g. painting parapets or changing bulbs in streetlights, are issues that should, amongst others, be addressed under CDM and the appropriate details recorded in the health and safety file.

Where safety-in-use is already the subject of existing legislation and Regulations, there is a temptation to include information regarding this in the health and safety file for this reason alone. The distinction between construction/maintenance/repair and safety-in-use must be made if the plan and the file are not to include unnecessary information.

Some of the authors found it difficult to distinguish between the construction/ maintenance/ repair aspect and the safety-in-use aspect, particularly where there already exists other legislation related to health and safety. This is a distinction that needs to be made if the plan and the file are not to include unnecessary information.

## 12.2.3  Reference to legislation

During the drafting of this report the HSE confirmed that it was not intended that health and safety plans should list every construction related Act of Parliament and Regulation. Specific legislation should be listed only where it applied to operations involving significant hazards, for example removal of asbestos. However, omission of reference to other legislation (which may in itself be a breach of the CDM Regulations) will not allow any contractor to plead ignorance of that legislation as a defence in any action arising from an incident.

## 12.2.4  Feasibility studies

In some situations the client may wish to have pre-feasibility and/or feasibility studies carried out to determine whether the project should proceed in the first place. It would be prudent for designers to take account of the CDM Regulations, and the needs of regulation 13 (Requirements on designers), during the feasibility process remembering that the lengths to which a designer has to go are qualified by what is reasonably practicable at the time the feasibility is carried out.

Likewise, designers should be careful not to progress feasibility studies too quickly to consider health and safety, with the danger of the client approving a scheme which then turns out to contain inherent risks to the health and safety of construction workers that cannot be avoided.

Designers should take steps to ensure that information generated during the feasibility stage is then retained to form the initial inputs into the health and safety plan and file, when a scheme is chosen and the project is confirmed.

## 12.2.5   Cross references in the plan and the file

It will have been seen from the examples that much of the information needed for the pre-tender stage health and safety plan and the health and safety file is already provided as part of the standard contract documentation, or is passed between the designer and the contractor.

It is not intended that all this existing documentation should be duplicated to meet the requirements of the health and safety plan. The plan is for passing information between parties and to be effective should be in the most readily understandable form. If this is determined to be through specifications, drawings or other material which has already been prepared and is on the record between the appropriate parties, this can then be cross referenced by the plan.

What is important is that the tender documentation, including the pre-tender stage health and safety plan, should be internally consistent and complete as a whole.

The health and safety file will eventually form part of the handover documentation to the client. Again it may be acceptable to cross refer to other handover documents, providing that all the documents are always kept together. If the handover documents are likely to be dispersed, the health and safety file should contain copies of all drawings, specifications, manuals etc. so that it is complete.

It is recognised that whereas the planning supervisor is only charged with ensuring that the health and safety plan is prepared, the actual task of collating the information provided by the design team into a coherent package will not be a trivial exercise and will require dedicated resources from whichever organisation is instructed to do it.

## 12.2.6   Level of detail in the plan

Under CDM it is not the function of the designer as such to prepare the plan nor to see that it is prepared. The designer in providing information about the design will, however, make a vital contribution, the plan being essentially about managing risks the designer could not avoid or reduce.

As has been said, designers can assume competence of the appointed contractors and the examples have been produced on this basis, taking account of the nature of the project. Designers do not, therefore, need to repeat in the plan information about matters which a competent contractor would be expected to consider in the ordinary course of his business.

This approach avoids the plan becoming severely overburdened with valid, but unnecessary details which could swamp and even mask information which the contractor did need to have drawn to his attention.

This understanding is spelt out in the Approved Code of Practice. This is a pragmatic approach by the Health and Safety Executive to the enforcement of the CDM Regulations. Judgements about whether in fact tendering contractors will be competent are matters for planning supervisors and clients. Relevant guidance is provided in *A guide to the managing of health and safety in construction*, which is a companion to *Designing for health and safety in construction*.

On simple projects especially, there may be a tendency to include more details in the health and safety plan than is necessary. The case study in Section 5 has shown that a health and safety plan can be a relatively short document.

### 12.2.7 The COSHH Regulations

The Control of Substances Hazardous to Health (COSHH) Regulations 1988 provide a comprehensive approach to the safe handling of a wide range of substances used in the workplace. They set out the essential measures needed to prevent or adequately control exposures to substances hazardous to health.

The regulations do not apply to construction designers in the act of designing. They require the avoidance and reduction of risk in the choice of materials and substances by contractors; but this does not relieve designers of their similar duties under CDM regulation 13. In passing on information about their designs, designers can assume possession of the relevant COSHH information by contractors, but applications in unusual circumstances, or requiring other than standard precautions, should certainly be noted and input provided to the health and safety plan and/or the file.

### 12.2.8 The health and safety file

The structure of the health and safety file has already been described in Section 2.8. Its statutory purpose is enable clients, their successors or tenants to pass information regarding the design and construction, maintenance, repair or demolition of the works to any persons who may work on the completed structure in the future.

The Regulations and ACOP state that the planning supervisor has the duty to ensure a health and safety file is prepared and then to review, amend or add to it as necessary. The planning supervisor is also responsible for ensuring delivery of the file to the client.

The manner in which the file is assembled is open. In terms of the Regulations, the file is not needed until the end of the construction phase when it is passed to the client by the planning supervisor. However, information to be included in the file will be generated throughout the design and construction of the works by many different contributors, including designers, contractors, specialist sub-contractors and suppliers.

It is suggested that the health and safety file might be compiled by putting all information flagged for the file to the planning supervisor or other designated party at agreed intervals throughout the project, who would then delete redundant or superseded information to keep the file current.

In addition to its statutory function, a health and safety file that is regularly reviewed throughout the design and construction stages will provide a record of the health and safety status quo of the project. Designers and planning supervisors may find it useful to have access to such a document, especially should work on the project be stopped and restarted for funding, planning permission or other reasons. Additionally, designers may wish to retain information arising from concept or scheme design etc. to be able to demonstrate at a later date that options were properly considered at the appropriate time.

### 12.2.9 Method statements and construction sequence

Method statements are usually prepared by contractors, sometimes on the instructions of the architect or engineer, to describe how a particular operation or piece of work is to be carried out. As such they almost always include a commentary on the health and safety of operatives and others.

It is stated within the ACOP (paragraph 68) that "the Regulations do not require architects and engineers ... to dictate construction methods". The Project Steering Group debated whether the Regulations may be interpreted as entailing any requirement for contractors to receive method statements from consultants. It was agreed that the present trend away from consultants providing formal method statements to contractors will not be affected.

However, the CDM Regulations will, through the health and safety plan, make information available to the contractor regarding the construction sequence that was assumed for the purposes of design, where this is unusual, innovative or outside the scope of a competent contractor. It would then be up to the contractor to propose an alternative method or sequence if he so wished, but in any event the contractor would remain responsible for health and safety on site during construction.

### 12.2.10 Dealing with previously made decisions

Some of the examples refer to matters decided before the designer was engaged. It should be borne in mind that this report was largely prepared before the Regulations were launched. Where, in accordance with the transitional arrangements for the coming into force of the Regulations, regulation 13 applies, it must be complied with. It is assumed that in such cases and in the future, the Regulations will have the same effect on clients' wishes as any other relevant legal requirement, for example those relating to planning.

It must be remembered that regulation 13 is about a balance of design considerations rather than a prescription that health and safety must prevail at the cost of all else. This flexibility makes the Regulations practicable but it does not appear that clients can make decisions that bind and/or restrict the designer without possibly attracting designers' duties to themselves.

# 13 Conclusions

Insofar as the subject matter of this study has been a set of proposed Regulations with associated Approved Code of Practice and HSE guidance, it is not possible to draw conclusions in the usual way.

This project has enabled eight designers to put forward their responses to the duties imposed by the CDM Regulations and to have these reviewed by a widely representative Steering Group, including the Health and Safety Executive and individuals with many years experience of health and safety practice. The Steering Group obtained significant concensus of opinion on the detail presented in the report.

The study has raised a number of issues which have been examined briefly in Section 12 and which it is hoped will be the subject of further debate and, if necessary, suitable clarification.

In discussion with members of the Steering Group, certain issues have been identified as subjects for further work by CIRIA and CIC, including a wider range of case studies and research to monitor the impact of the CDM Regulations on a live construction project.

# References

HMSO
*The Construction (Design and Management) Regulations 1994*
SI 1994/3140

*Managing construction for health and safety: Construction (Design and Management) Regulations 1994 Approved Code of Practice*
L54
HSE, 1995

*Designing for health and safety in construction*
HSE, 1995

*A guide to managing health and safety in construction*
HSE, 1995

HMSO
*The Management of Health and Safety at Work Regulations 1992*

*Five steps to risk assessment*
HSE, 1994

ST. J HOLT, A. and ANDREWS, H.
*Principles of health and safety at work*
Institute of Occupational Safety and Health, 1992

*Risk assessment - a practical guide*
The safety and health practitioners
IOSH, 1993

*Successful health and safety management*
HSE, HS(G)65, 1991

*A safer bet - an introduction to the principles of the CDM Regulations 1994* (video)
Construction Industry Council, 1995